GROW YOUR OWN

REBECCA DESNOS

Grow Your Own Colour is independently
published by Rebecca Desnos.

rebeccadesnos.com / info@rebeccadesnos.com

Instagram: @rebeccadesnos

Published by Rebecca Desnos, in 2023, in the UK

Copyright © Rebecca Desnos 2023

ISBN 978-1-7398197-4-3 (paperback)
ISBN 978-1-7398197-5-0 (eBook)

DISCLAIMER:

The publisher has made every effort to ensure
that all instructions given in this book are accurate
and safe, but they cannot accept liability, whether
direct or consequential and however arising.
The publisher does not accept liability for any
accidents, injuries, legal consequences or any other
damages incurred by any reader following the
information in this book.

Only gather plants that you can identify with 100%
certainty as some plants are toxic. Some of the
activities may be potentially toxic or hazardous
and you should take caution when carrying
out the projects. Children should have full adult
supervision if participating in any activities.

Please follow the safety guidelines in this book and
use your own common sense. Please seek health
and safety advice from a medical professional.

Hi! I'm Rebecca Desnos, a natural
dyer in the UK, a writer, mother,
and an all-round plant lover.

I'm an independent publisher who
is passionate about sharing a love
of plants with others!

Get in touch

Do you have any comments or questions?
I'd love to hear from you!

info@rebeccadesnos.com

Welcome!

Do you dream of bringing more creativity into your life? Do you love plants? Well, natural dyeing is the perfect combination for you and there's nothing more delightful than growing your own dye plants.

The plants in this book are a beautiful addition to any balcony or garden...

I used to always think that plants had to tick one of the following boxes in order to earn their place in my garden: edible, herbal or dye. But it's not that simple and there are many overlaps. Lots of edible herbs also make incredible dye, such as culinary herbs! Beautiful cutting flowers like cosmos and scabiosa also make gorgeous dye. And let's not forget the pollinators who will enjoy all types of blooms, so every flowering plant has some kind of use in the garden.

Within the next 130+ pages I've shared my tips for growing, harvesting and dyeing with my favourite dye plants. I hope you fill this book with lots of notes as you begin your journey to grow your own colour!

Rebecca x

Join my online class!

There's a video workshop that accompanies this book. Come along to my virtual studio and we'll make some beautiful colours together!

Sign up on **rebeccadesnos.com**.

CONTENTS

chilternseeds.co.uk

Chiltern Seeds

Cosmos sulphureus
"Cosmic" Series
"... Red"

Dyeing Crafts Seeds

Hopi Black Sunflower

www.dyeing-crafts.co.uk

Tagetes
"Konstance"

Chiltern Seeds

Ch

ds

DYERS
CAMOMILE

EARLY
SUNRISE
COREOPSIS

BAILIWICK
BLUE

Dyeing Crafts Seeds

French Marigold

www.dyeing-crafts.co.uk

Chiltern Seeds

Tagetes erecta
"Crackerjack" Mixed
African Marigold
12210

Half Hardy Annual

Sow indoors or under glass: Feb-Apr

Sow outdoors: May-Jun

Height: 90cm Spread: 30cm

Sow thinly. Barely sow into seed compost which is moist
but well-drained. Only just cover with soil. Exposure of
15-18°C or put in a warm place. Light is required for
germination. Germination takes: 5-14 days. Transplant
seedlings when large enough to handle. Pot/bottle and
plant out once danger of frost has passed. Space at 15-
20cm. Can be sown directly from May with 25cm spacing,
keep moist until germinated.

www.chilternseeds.co.uk

D

Cosmos

'Rubenza'

Milli Proust
flowers

Dyeing Crafts Seeds

Hollyhock

www.dyeing-crafts.co.uk

Chil

Ch

GROW YOUR OWN COLOUR

GROWING

Starting a dye garden

Is this your first time growing dye plants? Perhaps you already have a garden or balcony and would like to add some new plants into your growing space? There are many beautiful plants to choose from in this book that make wonderful additions to any vegetable or ornamental garden.

Planning your growing space

Before you sow any seeds, plan your growing space. Will you grow directly in the ground, in raised beds or in pots? Perhaps you'll use a mixture of all three options.

My current garden is fairly small. I live in the UK and my approximate USDA zone is 8-9 and I grow a mixture of dye plants, herbs, and a few vegetables. I always begin with detailed plans for where to plant things, but end up developing the garden in a more intuitive, flexible way.

Are you going to fit in some new dye plants amongst your vegetables? Maybe you'd like to grow cosmos in a pot? Or perhaps you'll transform a whole area into a dye garden.

Sourcing or making compost

You'll need compost for any type of growing, whether you grow in pots or in the ground. At the beginning, you'll need to buy compost, but perhaps you have space for a compost bin so you can make your own for future years. There are even small scale composting systems for balconies, such as bokashi (fermentation) bins.

In my small garden, I have a 'hot bin', which I've really enjoyed using. There's a stirring stick that I use to give it a mix fairly often and it's produced beautiful compost in only a few months. There are many other options for compost bins.

For starting seeds, it's best to buy compost. Your homemade compost may have weed seeds that are still viable, so these will germinate when you sow your dye plant seeds. Store-bought compost will have been heated to the necessary temperature to kill off weed seeds.

Using manure is another option, but you need to be certain what the animals have been fed. In the UK, many gardeners have accidentally used manure contaminated by aminopyralid. This herbicide is often sprayed onto crops, then fed to livestock and the chemicals end up in their manure. When contaminated manure is used in the garden, it severely affects the growth of plants. If you ever use manure in your garden, ensure that the animals were given organic feed only. (Richards, 2022).

Some principles to consider

If you're new to gardening, here are some ideas to think about when planning your growing space:

- **Sunlight:** Choose the sunniest spot for your dye plants. However, I've grown plants on a shady balcony with only afternoon sun, and things grew surprisingly well. Most plants prefer sunshine, but will tolerate some shade.

- **Height of plants:** Position the taller plants at the back of a bed. I plant Hopi Black Dye sunflowers at the back (tied into the fence to keep them upright), then medium height plants in front e.g. scabiosa, coreopsis, cosmos and Japanese indigo, followed by the smallest plants at the front, like French marigolds. Tall and floppy plants like coreopsis and scabiosa flowers may benefit from being loosely 'tied in' to avoid smothering other plants.

- **Repeat-flowering:** The flowers in this book are all "cut-and-come-again", so, the more you pick, the more dye material you'll get. It's important to pick flowers regularly, as this signals to the plant to grow more. If you let flowers begin to go to seed, this will slow down the production of new flowers. It's possible to get a surprisingly large amount of dye material from a small space. It's hard to predict exactly how much, as this depends on the soil fertility, level of sunlight, overall weather, water and other factors.

Glossary of plant terms

Hardy annuals e.g. scabiosa.

These are the most cold-tolerant annuals. They live for one year, forming roots, leaves, flowers and seeds all within 12 months. A seedling that germinates in the late summer or early autumn will then go into a semi-dormant state through the winter, coming into growth again the following spring. When a heavy frost is forecast, these plants will need to be protected with horticultural fleece.

Half-hardy annuals e.g. sunflowers, marigolds, coreopsis & cosmos.

These plants cannot withstand winter wet and cold and will be killed by frost. Sow the seeds in little pots or module trays and keep them indoors or in a greenhouse, protecting them until the frosts are over. Grow for a few weeks under cover, then they will be ready to go out in the garden at the end of spring. These plants will be killed by the frosts in the autumn.

Tender annuals e.g. Japanese indigo.

These plants are native to tropical regions and are easily damaged by the cold and will be killed by frosts. They are more sensitive than half-hardy annuals.

Biennials e.g. hollyhock.

These plants form roots and leaves in the first year, then flower and set seed the following summer, after which they die.

Perennials e.g. dyer's chamomile & chocolate cosmos.

These plants will live for more than one year. Half-hardy perennials (dyer's chamomile) will survive winter frosts, whereas tender perennials (chocolate cosmos) need to be dug up and brought inside to protect from frost.

Photo on the left: *African marigold, cosmos rubenza and Japanese indigo, growing alongside black cornflowers, which can also be used for dye but aren't as potent as purple pincushion flowers.*

Sowing seeds

When it comes to sowing seeds, here are a couple of options:

1. **Sow seeds directly in the ground** after your last frost, once the ground has warmed up.

2. **Sow in little pots or modules indoors** 6-8 weeks before your last frost date.

When to start your seeds

- Your seed packets will probably give an indication of when to sow seeds, but it may not be accurate for your local area and climate. You need to know your last predicted spring frost date, which you can find by looking online. Look at *plantmaps.com* and zoom in to your area and see the last predicted frost date for your exact location.

- Hardy annuals can be sown indoors 6-8 weeks before the last frost, then planted in the garden after the last frost. Half-hardy annuals are best started a bit later when the day and night temperatures don't fluctuate so much. Don't rush, as seeds sown later will often make healthier plants. Tender annuals should be planted out later as these are the most sensitive to the cold. If you live in a warmer climate, your growing season will be longer, so you can be more flexible with planting dates.

- Grow a few more seedlings than you need, in case there are any disasters when they are planted out, such as an unexpected frost or damage from creatures. If necessary, you can swap in the spare plants.

Benefits of starting seeds in modules

- You'll get a few extra weeks of growing time in comparison to direct sowing, so your plants will flower earlier.

- By the time the plants go out in the garden, they'll be more resilient to any pests that try to nibble on the leaves. Seedlings have delicate stems which a slug can easily munch straight through, instantly killing the plant.

- You can easily keep a close eye on germination and clearly see which seeds have and haven't germinated, and resow if necessary.

- Out in the garden, sometimes it is hard to tell what is a weed and what is your intended plant. When you put larger plants in the garden, there's no mistaking the difference.

- If you have animals in your garden (pets or wild), then there's always the risk that they will walk over or dig in your beds after you've sown seeds, totally messing up everything. However, you can use netting to protect your beds if you like.

Dyer's chamomile grown in cardboard tubes in a recycled plastic tub

Check the germination rate of your seeds

You may choose to do this if your seeds are more than a year old. Sprinkle 25 seeds in a zigzag pattern onto a damp paper towel, roll up and place in a plastic ziplock bag. Place in a warm place and leave for a week or so. Then take a look and count how many seeds have germinated. Multiply this number by four and this will give you the percentage of germination. If your germination rate is quite low, you can always sow more seeds to compensate, or buy fresh seeds.

Choosing module trays or paper pots

- You can use plastic module trays which last several years. Treat each cell in the tray as a mini pot.

- Make your own paper pots using a wooden tool. Look online for "paper pot maker".

- Make your own mini pots using cardboard tubes packed neatly into a larger tray. This is my favourite method and I save cardboard tubes all year (they are easier to store pressed flat). Simply cut each tube in half, place in a larger dish or tray, then fill with compost quite firmly. Treat each of the tubes as a little pot. When it comes to planting out in the garden, bury the cardboard tubes, as they will decompose in the ground over the next few months.

Seedlings need a lot of sunlight to grow

- Around Valentine's Day, in the middle of February, the daylight starts to exceed ten hours a day and continues to increase day by day, until the summer solstice in June. Ten hours is the minimum number of hours that most plants need in order to grow, so don't start any seeds before then.

- Seedlings require a lot of light to grow well. They can be grown on a sunny indoor windowsill, but it often won't offer adequate sunlight and the seedlings will become "leggy", which means they grow elongated stems in search of light.

- To avoid growing leggy seedlings, you can use LED grow lights indoors, but there is the added cost of electricity with this option. Or you can put your trays of seedlings in a greenhouse or cold-frame outside. Until nighttime temperatures go above 10°C, I bring my seedlings into the house at night, then return them to the greenhouse each morning. Or you can cover them with fleece for insulation.

- If you do end up with leggy seedlings, then you can rectify this by transferring each seedling into a new module or pot and bury the stem so that the leaves are at the compost level. Make sure that the seedlings get enough light from now on so they don't develop elongated stems again. (Note: Hollyhock will be stunted if its roots are disturbed and it won't continue to grow.)

How to sow seeds in modules

Note: Sunflower seeds are best sown in larger pots as they grow very quickly. All the other plants in this book can be grown in module trays or small paper pots.

1. Choose the container(s) you'll use: a module tray, paper pots or cardboard tubes. For paper pots and cardboard tubes, put these into a tray. Keep on adding more until they fill the space of the tray and don't move around. If you use a plastic module tray, place it into a larger tray (they often come in sets so you can get a tray that fits perfectly underneath).

2. Fill the modules or individual pots with compost. If you're using paper pots or cardboard tubes, pack in the compost well and top up until they are filled right to the top. You can even fill compost into the gaps between tubes (see photo on page 15), which keeps things really secure and stops the tubes from moving around.

3. Water the compost before sowing any seeds. If you water afterwards, then the water will displace your seeds.

4. Add a couple of seeds per module or pot. For smaller seeds, just drop the seeds onto the surface of the compost, then lightly cover with a dusting of compost, or vermiculite if you prefer. For larger seeds like cosmos and marigold, poke the seeds vertically into the compost. For marigolds, notice that one end of the seed is dark, and this should be pointing downwards into the compost (see photo on page 28).

5. Seeds need moisture and warmth to germinate. One option is to place your tray into a plastic bag and make a few holes in the bag for air flow. The bag is a make-shift propagator and creates a warm, damp microclimate, but isn't absolutely necessary. Whether or not you use a plastic bag, place the tray somewhere warm in the house to help the seeds germinate. Check on them every day, and they should sprout after a few days. Some will take longer to germinate and others may even take a few weeks. You can also place trays onto electric heat mats for a few days to speed up germination (this is especially helpful with Japanese indigo).

6. When your seeds have germinated, they will need maximum sunlight to grow, so take the plastic bag off and put them in the brightest place.

7. You can water the tray below so the compost absorbs the moisture and the roots drink it up. Or water from above using a fine rose watering can.

8. You may choose to 'pot on' some of the seedlings into larger pots if it looks like they are outgrowing their current pots or modules.

9. Allow the seedlings to grow for 6-8 weeks, until the temperatures are high enough for them to survive outside. Japanese indigo is particularly susceptible to the cold, as it's a semi-tropical plant, so wait until it's much warmer before you plant out those seedlings.

On my balcony in a previous home,
I grew Coreopsis grandiflora &
Persicaria tinctoria in pots.

Growing in pots

Don't have a garden but dream of growing dye plants? Don't let your lack of space stop you!

Before I had a garden, I mainly dyed with foraged plants and grew a few potted plants on my balcony. The balcony was north-west facing and only had direct sun after 2pm and things grew surprisingly well. If you have less than ideal growing conditions, you might be amazed by how well your plants do.

For a balcony garden, think about growing multipurpose plants such as herbs, as these can be used for dyeing as well as in your culinary creations. Sage is one of my favourite multipurpose plants – it's beautiful to look at, edible, medicinal and a dye plant! When we print plants onto fabric through hammering or bundle dyeing, the dye is transferred directly onto the fabric, so we can get away with using just a handful of leaves or flowers. You get maximum impact from very few plants! Ink-making is another great option for small projects.

On my balcony I liked to use fabric pots made from recycled plastic bottles. They are affordable and most importantly light enough to move around the balcony. You can use a whole variety of pots and containers, but of course the best option is to simply use what you already have on hand. Fill your pots with compost and your balcony garden is all set. Keep in mind that pots need regular watering and dry out quickly in the sun.

Growing in the ground

When growing plants in the garden, there are many options such as using raised beds or growing directly in the ground. In my current garden, I've chosen to grow in the ground because I like the flexibility this method offers. This way, you can change the growing space and pathways whenever you like. I've even extended my growing space by laying down more cardboard over the lawn, which I'll show you in a moment. Also you don't need much compost to get started, whereas filling raised beds would call for a larger volume.

Have you heard of no-dig gardening?

Over the past few years, I've followed no-dig gardening principles, in particular Charles Dowding's teachings. Crucially, the ground is left undisturbed and we never "dig in" compost to enrich the soil. Instead, add a layer of compost mulch onto the soil surface once a year. This applies to growing in raised beds too; just sprinkle the compost onto the surface.

To create no-dig beds on lawn, it's as simple as covering the grass with something opaque to exclude light (cardboard is commonly used) and this helps the grass die off within a few months. After laying down cardboard, top with a layer of compost and you can plant into your new bed immediately. It's a simple way to create an instant garden! The next couple of pages have all the details and you'll see just how easy it is!

So, why no-dig? Apart from saving a lot of time and energy, no-dig gardening helps produce healthier soil as the soil life isn't disturbed by digging. Soil isn't just "dirt" like we've been led to believe; it contains a network of microscopic fungi between soil particles, roots and rocks. The no-dig method keeps these fungi networks complete.

Fungi perform important roles in the soil involving:

- **Decomposition**: Along with bacteria, fungi play an important role in decomposing plant matter. They convert hard-to-digest organic material into forms that other organisms can use.

- **Water retention**: Some fungi physically bind soil particles together, which means the soil can hold more water. As a result, no dig beds often require less frequent watering than gardens that are dug over.

- **Nutrients**: Many plants depend on fungi to help extract nutrients from the soil. No-dig gardening produces healthier and stronger plants.

GROW YOUR OWN COLOUR

How to make a no-dig garden bed

- Collect large boxes – standard brown corrugated cardboard, not shiny boxes. Remove any plastic tape and collapse them. Add to your cardboard collection gradually, or ask any local shops if they have spare boxes. If the tape is difficult to remove, you can do this step just before you use them in the garden; allow the boxes to get wet in the rain (or spray with a hose) and the tape will peel off easily.

- Buy compost (ideally organic) or use your homemade compost.

- Measure the lawn and mark out the size of bed you'd like to make, and lay cardboard down. Make sure you overlap the sheets carefully; the aim is to exclude all light from the grass so it is killed off.

- Water the cardboard thoroughly so it is soaking wet. Wet cardboard is easier to plant into if you need to cut through it to plant in the ground below, and it's also less likely to blow away.

- Top the cardboard with a layer of compost and walk over it to firm down. (This is called the *No-Dig Dance* by many!) There isn't a definitive amount of compost that you need. I've made beds with as little as 5cm depth of compost and some with 10cm. Generally, the more compost you use, the better, but be assured that it's still possible with less.

- The cardboard will decompose over the next few months. Worms enjoy eating it and will mix it into the soil.

- It can be helpful to place lengths of wood along the edges of the bed to hold down the cardboard until it has fully decomposed, then remove after a few months. This will give a neater edge but it's not absolutely necessary.

- Every year, top the bed with 2-3cm of compost. This adds nourishment back into the soil. Worms will mix it in over time, and crucially the network of fungi are undisturbed and allowed to thrive. With this method, no other fertiliser is needed; the compost is packed full of nutrients.

Planting into your new bed

- You can sow seeds or plant seedlings straight into your new garden bed.

- To plant seedlings, use a 'dibber' or small trowel to make holes and plant directly into the top layer of compost. If the compost layer is very shallow, you'll need to dig down through the layer of cardboard and into the ground below. Watering the cardboard beforehand makes it easier to pierce and dig through. Add some extra compost around the stems of the plants to ensure the grass is smothered and the light is excluded.

Planting your seedlings & nurturing your garden

When your seedlings have been growing for 6-8 weeks, and your last frost date has passed, check the weather forecast for the next few days to make sure a frost isn't expected.

Each of the dye plants has its own section later in the book with growing notes, so refer to these sections for detailed instructions.

Planting out your seedlings

If your seedlings have been cocooned inside your home for their whole life, then it's a good idea to "harden them off" which means putting the baby plants outside for a few hours a day, gradually building up to longer. The theory is that a sudden change in temperature can shock the young plants.

Another option is to cover a new bed of plants with a sheet of horticultural fleece. Not only does this shield young plants from the wind, but it also protects them from creatures. I had the unfortunate experience of witnessing almost an entire bed of plants being stolen by birds within the first 24 hours of planting out. *(Oh, the horror!)* So I think I'll always use fleece over my beds for the first couple of weeks, to give the roots time to establish, so birds can't simply lift them out of the ground.

Slug & snail deterrents

If you live in a damp country like the UK, then you're likely to have a lot of slugs and snails living in your garden. Some plants, especially sunflowers, make a very tasty treat, and before long, all the leaves will be gone and the plant will die.

Most people know the dangers of using toxic slug and snail pellets, so try this natural option instead. Surround the base of your sunflowers with a "fence" of prickly bramble stems – slugs and snails won't be able to slither over the thorns. I find that I have to add extra brambles a couple of times, but I'm able to deter the slugs enough so the plants continue to grow. As the plants mature, they will be resilient enough to survive the odd nibble here and there. With this method, you're not eliminating nature from your garden, but you're growing alongside it.

Even though slugs and snails can be annoying in our gardens, they actually play an important role in the ecosystem. Interestingly, in 2022, the Royal Horticultural Society declassified slugs and snails as pests: *"...the slimy creatures are misunderstood, as only nine of the 44 recognised species of slug in the UK eat garden plants[...] Slugs are nature's recyclers [...] clearing dead matter from the garden, and are also important food for more beloved garden guests including hedgehogs and birds. Some species even get rid of algae from greenhouses."* (Horton, 2022).

Watering

Try to water in the early mornings. If you water later in the day when it's very warm, the water will evaporate before it's had the chance to fully soak into the soil. If you water at night and live in a slug-prone area, then you'll create the perfect damp environment to attract these slimy critters. These are just guidelines and of course it's not always possible to follow exactly.

Frequent harvesting

You can prolong the blooming period of your plants by deadheading any flowers that have gone over. Of course it's best to harvest your flowers before this point, but if any go to seed, then this signals to the plant that the growing period is coming to an end, and the plant will put its energy into producing seeds, rather than new buds. The good news is that the more flowers you harvest for dyeing, the more flowers you'll get.

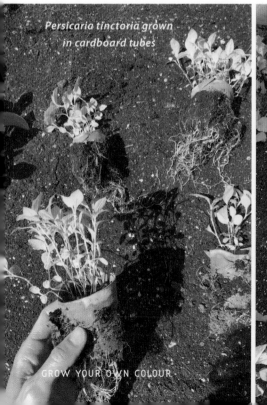

Persicaria tinctoria grown in cardboard tubes

GROW YOUR OWN COLOUR

Harvesting & drying flowers

The flowers in this book are all "cut-and-come-again", which means the more you pick, the more they will bloom. Don't feel like you're wasting flowers by picking them regularly. Use as many fresh flowers as you like in your projects, then dry the rest so you can carry on with your dye projects in the winter. Use dried flowers in dye pots, to make ink, or sprinkle onto fabric for bundle dyeing. You'll find all of these projects later in the book.

To dry flowers, spread them across plates or racks (racks provide more air circulation) and allow them to air dry fully before storing in paper bags or jars. Use the same principles as drying herbs for making tea: dry out of sunlight to preserve the colours and make sure the plants are as dry as a crisp before storing, otherwise they will turn mouldy. You can also press flowers to use in bundle dye projects and make more precise prints.

When dyeing with fresh plants, use the general guide of 1:1 plants to fabric; weigh your dry fabric and use the same weight of flowers. Broadly speaking, dried flowers will make a less intense dye than fresh. It's not as simple as using twice the amount of dried plants as fresh. This is because dried plants are a limited resource. We can only dry a finite amount of plants in the summer months, so if we use vast amounts in our winter dye pots, then our store will soon be gone. This is why bundle dyeing is such a special method – just a handful of flowers will have a big impact.

French
marigold

Dyer's coreopsis

Coreopsis tinctoria
'radiata tigrina'

Hopi Black Dye
sunflower

Sulphur cosmos

Purple
pincushion

Seed saving

It's so rewarding to collect your own seeds from homegrown flowers. It's as simple as letting some of the flowers mature fully and 'go to seed'. Then pick the flower heads, shake out the seeds, allow them to dry, then store in little paper envelopes. Label them with the name and date. Most seeds will be viable for a year or two, but fresh seeds always give the best germination rates, so try to use them the next season. (Refer to page 16 to see how to check the germination rate of your stored seeds.) Store your seeds out of direct sunlight in a cool area of your home, or you can refrigerate them.

Cross-pollination

Many flowers will cross-pollinate which means your saved seeds are unlikely to give you the exact same flowers the following year. When you save the seeds of a cross-pollinated plant and grow these the following year, those flowers could look different because the two parent plants weren't of the same variety. Cross-pollination only occurs between members of the same botanical species.

For flowers like coreopsis and marigold, this doesn't matter too much, as they are all yellow, red or orange and produce dye. However, it can be frustrating with other plants. Sunflowers are cross-pollinated, so your Hopi Black Dye sunflowers may well cross-pollinate with other local sunflowers. This means that next year's sunflower seeds probably won't be as dark.

You can't guarantee what next year's flowers will look like, but on the other hand, it's a lovely surprise to see the variations in your homegrown flowers, especially if you're growing flowers for pure joy and to use in floral arrangements.

It's important to know about cross-pollination if you share seeds with others, and especially if you plan to sell them. If you allow your flowers to cross-pollinate, then there's no knowing exactly what your saved seeds will grow. To guarantee what your flowers will look like, it's best to buy seeds each year from a reputable seller. Flower growers and seed sellers have ways of isolating flowers in poly tunnels or netting to guarantee that plants won't cross-pollinate.

For detailed information on saving seeds, you'll love *The Complete Guide to Seed Saving* by Gough and Moore-Gough. The book lists every vegetable, herb and flower imaginable, with details on germination, growing, flowering, pollination and seed collection. For example, these are the isolation requirements to avoid cross-pollination of marigolds: *"[Marigolds] are normally cross-pollinated and should be isolated by about 1/4 mile between varieties of the same species..."*

DYE PLANTS

GROW YOUR OWN COLOUR

Hopi Black Dye Sunflowers

The hulls of Hopi Black Dye sunflower seeds are black and they produce a stunning array of colours. Sunflowers are one of the oldest domesticated crops from North America (believed to originate as early as 3,600 BC) and the Hopi Black variety *(Helianthus annuus macrocarpus)* was bred and selected over many generations for its dark pigmented and large edible seeds.

Known as *Tceqa' Qu' Si* in Hopi, these black sunflower seeds make a traditional dye used in Hopi basketry and wool dyeing. The Hopi Tribe is a sovereign nation located in northeastern Arizona. As of the 2010 census, there were over 19,000 Hopi in the United States.

The colours possible from Hopi Black Dye sunflower seeds include maroon, dark purple, lavender, mid blue, grey and black. According to *nativeseeds.org*, to achieve a deep purple dye, alum is used as a mordant, traditionally from efflorescence of drying soil. To produce a black dye for basketry, iron from yellow ochre, as well as piñon gum (resin from piñon pine trees) is added to the dye.

Growing

The clue is in the name – sunflowers will want as much sun as possible, but they also like some shelter from wind. Make sure you plant your sunflowers at the back of a border otherwise they will overshadow everything else.

You can either sow indoors in small pots a few weeks before your last predicted frost date, or sow direct in the ground or in large pots after the last frost. Sow more seeds than you need so you can select the best ones for dye. According to Grand Prismatic Seed (seed supplier in the US), the colour of the stem correlates to the seed colour, so keep the dark pigmented seedling stems and remove the green ones. This will give you the best chance of growing sunflowers with the darkest black seed hulls for dyeing. Aim for one sunflower growing every couple of feet, or one per large pot.

In cooler climates such as the UK, you can start your seeds indoors and plant outside a few weeks later. This gives you the best chance of your sunflowers producing flowers early. They will need repotting after a couple of weeks as they grow quickly. When you plant them in the garden, dig a hole that is larger than the pot, and bury it deep and top up with some extra compost. Water your sunflowers regularly.

If you're in a slug-prone area, you may need to use some kind of slug deterrent. My favourite method is to surround the bases of the stems with thorny brambles so the slugs can't slither over the barrier and reach the plants, as described on page 24. When I first tried this, I found that it didn't work 100% and one out six plants was still eaten somewhat, but incredibly this particular plant grew faster than the slugs could eat the leaves and it thrived all summer. This ended up being the strongest, tallest plant. This experience showed me that it's truly possible to respect wildlife and not resort to killing anything.

The flower heads become very heavy and can drag down the whole plant, so give the plants some support, such as tying the stems to a fence (see photo opposite). To do this, simply screw D-rings to the fence and thread wide strips of fabric through the metal rings and gently pass this around the front of the stems, then thread back through the ring and then tie a knot in the fabric. This gives the plants plenty of support as they grow.

Each plant grows multiple flower heads which is spectacular to see. At one point I spotted over 50 flowers growing from six plants!

Sunflower heads are a natural bird feeder with hundreds of tasty seeds. You might find that birds peck away at the seeds, so you can tie lightweight cotton muslin around the biggest flower heads to allow the seeds to mature before harvesting them.

Hopi Black Dye Sunflower (Helianthus annuus macrocarpus)

- Half-hardy annual
- Height: 2 - 3 m
- Planting distance: 60 cm
- Sow: Under cover in early to mid spring, or direct after last frost
- Position: full sun
- Flowers: mid to late summer

Harvesting

Once a flower has finished blooming, the petals will begin to shrivel up. To check if the seeds are ripe enough, see if they are black and shiny. Rub your fingers over the seeds to see if they stain your skin purple. This is a good indication that the flowers are ready to harvest.

Cut each head a few inches down the stem. Remove the seeds from the flower heads using a fork and either dry the seeds for later use, or dye with them straight away. All sunflower seeds are edible so you can of course eat the insides and save the shells for dyeing.

The heads can be dried for a couple of weeks as this makes it slightly easier to remove the seeds. However, if you store the sunflower heads for too long, they will go mouldy; for long term storage, it's best to store the seeds loose.

Dye notes

The seeds are rich in anthocyanins, which is sensitive to heat, so never boil the dye. Instead, steep the seeds in hot water. Weigh your fabric and aim for 1:1 ratio of fabric to seeds. Less seeds will give you a lighter colour. Cover the seeds with hot (not boiling water) and allow them to soak for a few hours. Stir every so often. Add a small piece of fabric to the dye and keep an eye on the developing colour. You can heat the dye pot to keep the water warm, but don't boil. Soak the seeds for a few hours or over night.

When you're happy with the dye colour, strain out the dye and put the seeds aside. You can try doing a second dye extraction from the same seeds. Then wipe out your dye pot, as the seeds leave sticky deposits on the sides of the pot which can then mark your fabric. Pour the dye back into the clean pot, before adding fabric.

The best colours develop on the fabric when it's left to soak in the dye over night. Reheat the dye pot a few times (don't boil), and keep the lid on to keep in the heat. See page 94 for a simple dye pot recipe and further suggestions.

The dye is pH sensitive, which means it reacts to acids and alkalis. You can use this to your advantage by doing a final rinse in water with either lemon or vinegar for acid, and bicarbonate of soda (baking soda) for alkali. The acidic water will turn the fabric lilac, and the alkali will shift the colour to brown. Rinsing in plain tap water is likely to shift the colour to blue/grey, which is beautiful in its own right. If you do an acid or alkali rinse, you'll need to do this each time you wash the fabric.

You can also dip the fabric into weak iron water to darken the shade, which has the added benefit of improving colour fastness (see page 104).

Photo on the opposite page: *The fabric swatches were rinsed in water that had its pH level altered by: bicarbonate of soda (bottom left) and vinegar (right). The fabric in the centre was rinsed in plain tap water. Note how the cellulose fabric modified with bicarbonate of soda is brown, whereas the ribbon made from silk is blue.*

Marigolds

You might already be growing these cheerful flowers in your garden. Marigolds are often planted alongside vegetables, especially tomatoes, as their spicy fragrance is said to repel aphids and other pests. Why not try this multi-purpose plant in your dye pot? The more flowers you harvest, the more the plants will produce, and your marigolds are likely to bloom all summer and autumn! Marigolds add a happy pop of colour to any garden.

There are several types of marigold and here are two that I've grown. Each of these come in different types with different colours and patterned petals.

- *Tagetes patula,* commonly known as **French marigold**, is a small, low growing plant that gardeners often grow alongside vegetables and herbs (companion planting).

- *Tagetes erecta,* also known as **African, Mexican or Aztec marigold**, is a much taller plant than French marigold and the flowers are spectacular and offer a lot of plant material for dyeing.

Tagetes patula

Tagetes erecta

French marigold
(Tagetes patula)

- Half-hardy annual
- Height: 15 - 30 cm
- Planting distance: 30 cm
- Sow: Under cover in early spring, or direct after last frost
- Position: full sun
- Flowers: early summer to autumn

African or Aztec marigold
(Tagetes erecta)

- Half-hardy annual
- Height: 30 - 100 cm
- Planting distance: 45 cm
- Sow: Under cover in early spring, or direct after last frost
- Position: full sun
- Flowers: early summer to autumn

Vibrant dye from yellow
Tagetes erecta blooms

Growing

Marigolds are frost sensitive, so start them off indoors and plant out after the risk of frost has passed. By starting them earlier, you'll get flowers as early as June. Alternatively sow seeds directly outside after the last frost, but these will bloom later.

Refer to pages 14-17 for detailed notes on growing from seed.

The leaves of some varieties of marigold, and especially the plant sap, can cause rashes and blisters (phototoxic contact dermatitis) on people with sensitive skin if exposed to the sun after contact with the plant. It is therefore best to always wear gloves when planting and tending to marigolds.

Harvesting

When the flowers are fully open, they are ready to harvest. *Tagetes patula* only needs 50-60 days to flower, but *Tagetes erecta* is a more substantial plant and may need up to 100 days to bloom.

Cut the flowers individually and either dye with the fresh flowers, or dry to use later on. To dry, spread them out onto trays, or string onto a fine cotton thread and hang to dry. This doubles up as a decorative garland.

GROW YOUR OWN COLOUR

Above & opposite page: fabric dyed with yellow Tagetes erecta

Fabric dyed with Tagetes patula flowers

Dye notes

As with all flower dyes, generally the brightest colours are produced with lower heat, whilst allowing the flowers to steep in the dye bath for longer, as if making a strong cup of tea. Add in a small piece of fabric to monitor the dye colour. See page 94 for a simple dye pot recipe.

Different colour blooms will produce different shades of dye. Incredibly, yellow *Tagetes erecta* flowers make the most stunning green dye in an aluminium pot. The colour isn't quite as intense in a stainless steel pot.

Orange and red *Tagetes patula* produce bright yellow dye, sometimes with a hint of green.

There are so many factors that influence the final colour, so your flowers might produce different shades. Some of the factors include soil, climate, maturity of the flower, water, the mordant you use, and the temperature of the dye. Some dyes gradually oxidise over the course of hours and the dye colour will shift and change.

GROW YOUR OWN COLOUR

Anthemis tinctoria /
Cota tinctoria

- Short-lived perennial
- Height: 60 - 90 cm
- Planting distance: 30 cm
- Sow: Under cover in mid
  spring, or direct sow later
  in spring. Alternatively, sow
  in autumn and they will
  flower the next year
- Position: full sun
- Flowers: summer to
  autumn

Dyer's chamomile

Dyer's chamomile, also known as golden marguerite, yellow chamomile, oxeye daisy, and many other names, is a member of the sunflower family *(Asteraceae)*. There are many sub-species and hybrids that have different characteristics, such as 'Sauce Hollandaise' and 'E.C. Bruxton', which both have pale yellow petals, and 'Kelwayi' with deep yellow petals, but they all make yellow dye.

This sprawling, daisy-like plant is a bright and sunny addition to the garden, it's very low maintenance and produces lots of flowers. It's a short-lived perennial and usually dies after a couple of years.

It's a traditional source of yellow used in Europe, and is particularly useful for making green, when over dyed with indigo (as shown below).

Dyer's Chamomile *(Anthemis tinctoria* or *Cota tinctoria)* is different from the medicinal types: German Chamomile *(Matricaria recutita)* and Roman Chamomile *(Anthemis nobilis)*. Those types of chamomile can also be used for dye but are unlikely to produce such bright shades.

Pictured: Green cotton (on the left) was dyed with dyer's chamomile &
Japanese indigo. Yellow fabric (in the middle) is cotton, and the ribbon is silk.

Growing

Sow seeds in module trays or little pots in the early spring. After a few weeks, transplant the seedlings into the ground, or balcony planters (as shown in the photo on the left). They are quite hardy and can be planted out before the risk of frost has passed.

See pages 14-17 for detailed notes on growing from seed.

Dyer's chamomile self-seeds but the tender leaves of the tiny plants are susceptible to being eaten by slugs. To ensure your plants are more resilient against slugs, it's best to start from seed indoors and plant out larger plants. Cut back after flowering to encourage new growth from the base.

Dyer's chamomile growing in a pot on my old balcony

Harvesting

Pick the flower heads once they are just past their prime. As with some other members of the *Asteraceae* family, you'll see the middle of the flower grow larger as it matures. The yellow centre of the flower is actually made up of hundreds of tiny "disc florets" which are actually individual flowers. The yellow petals around the edge are "ray florets" and form a ring around the disc florets. Can you see in the photo above that some of the flowers have circles in the middle where some of the disc florets haven't opened yet? Every day or so, you'll see the circle in the centre get smaller as more of these tiny disc florets open and the middle "fills in". Wait until all of these have developed and opened before picking, as this will give you the most dye material.

Dye notes

The flowers can be used fresh or dry in the dye pot, as well as in bundle dyeing. They dry spectacularly well and the vibrant, almost acid yellow dye gives quite an energy boost in the winter months. See page 94 for a simple dye pot recipe.

The clear, bright dye is beautiful for layering with indigo to make stable green dyes (see pages 47 and 103). When the yellow fabric is dipped into iron water, it shifts the dye to a deep, chocolate brown. See the photo opposite and find instructions on page 104,

Brown fabric was dyed with dyer's chamomile & dipped in iron water

Coreopsis tinctoria

Coreopsis tinctoria *'Radiata Tigrina'*

Coreopsis grandiflora

GROW YOUR OWN COLOUR

Coreopsis

Coreopsis, also known as tickseed, is a beautiful plant to add to any garden. It comes in many varieties and some are annuals and some perennials. Coreopsis is in the *Asteraceae* (daisy and sunflower) family.

Perennial varieties include the large-headed *Coreopsis grandiflora*, which have a long flowering period and produce a lot of dye material. I grew these on my balcony for a few years and felt that they maximised the small growing space as they produced flowers so abundantly. Perennial coreopsis plants are long-flowering, but short-lived, and survive for around 3 years.

Annual varieties include dyer's coreopsis *(Coreopsis tinctoria)* which originates from North America and 'Radiata Tigrina', which grows as a smaller bush and has mottled petals. There are countless other varieties and they all contain dye.

Coreopsis was one of the sources of yellow dye used by pre-Columbian civilisations in central and southern America. (Cardon, 2007). The plants are rich in flavanoids; the flowers and plant tops can be used for dye.

Growing

Annual and perennial coreopsis are both easy to grow from seed. You can often find perennial coreopsis in garden centres which is very handy for an instant dye garden!

Sow annual coreopsis seeds directly in the ground after the last frost, or sow indoors in pots in the early spring ready to plant out after the last predicted frost date. Read pages 14-17 for detailed notes on growing from seed. In warmer climates, coreopsis self-seeds prolifically.

Coreopsis tinctoria

- Half-hardy annual
- Height: 30 - 60 cm (depending on variety)
- Planting distance: 30 - 45 cm (depending on variety)
- Sow: Under cover in mid spring, or direct after last frost
- Position: full sun
- Flowers: midsummer to autumn

Coreopsis are sun-loving plants and grow best with 6+ hours of sunshine, but I did grow a couple of perennial varieties with success on my shady balcony (with sun in the afternoon), so it's always worth trying to see how they grow for you. Don't let the rules put you off; try for yourself as you might be surprised.

Harvesting

Pick the flowers when they are in full bloom, or as they are beginning to go over. Harvest slowly and carefully so you don't accidentally pick any flower buds.

Pick the flowers before they begin to go to seed as it will stimulate the plant to grow more buds. As with many plants, the more you pick, the more you'll get.

Either dye with the fresh blooms straight from the garden, or dry them for later use. They also press well and are great printed onto fabric in bundle dyeing. They can be stored in their dry form for a few years and still produce potent dye.

Dye notes

Coreopsis is highly pH sensitive, and the colours will shift depending on the acidity. The orange dye turns acid yellow with the addition of vinegar or lemon juice, and shifts to red with bicarbonate of soda (baking soda). See page 99 for a demonstration of this.

After you've dyed your fabric, rinse out the excess dye, wash it, then do one final rinse in pH modified water to shift the orange colour to yellow or red. You'll need to do this each time you wash your fabric to return it to the desired shade.

It's fun having colour-changing clothes, but also frustrating, as clothing will very easily change if it's splashed with citrus juice, and it will be sensitive to sweat. For clothing, I find it more practical to use coreopsis in bundle dyeing or plant pounding, where you're not aiming for a uniform colour and any pH changes are less noticeable and can be embraced as part of the pattern.

Dye from *Coreopsis tinctoria*

Cosmos sulphureus

- Half-hardy annual
- Height: 0.3 m - 1.2 m (depending on variety)
- Planting distance: 40 cm
- Sow: Under cover in mid spring, or direct after last frost
- Position: full sun
- Flowers: midsummer to first frost

'Cosmic Red' (above left) and 'Cosmic Orange' (above right and opposite)

Sulphur cosmos

Sulphur cosmos, also known as yellow or orange cosmos, is a member of the *Asteraceae* family. These brightly coloured flowers will add sunny glow to your garden.

Cosmos sulphureus is available in yellow, orange and scarlet shades. There are many varieties such as 'Cosmic Orange', 'Cosmic Red', 'Limara Lemon' and 'Polidor', which are semi-double flowers. They each make slightly different dye colours which will be noticeable in bundle dyeing, but you may choose to mix them in a dye pot.

These are very free-flowering plants, and with regular picking, they continue to flower abundantly until the first frost. The plants are quite compact and stocky, with lots of branches. The stems are beautiful in floral displays, and the blooms dry and press well for winter dye projects.

Growing

Start the seeds in modules several weeks before the last frost. Then transfer the seedlings into larger pots and grow on for a few weeks, until it's time to plant them in the garden in the late spring, when all danger of frost has passed. Read pages 14-17 for detailed notes on growing from seed.

Harvesting

They will bloom prolifically from the summer into the late autumn, until the first frost, at which point the plants will die. Harvest the flowers regularly throughout the growing season; as with the other dye flowers in this book, picking them will encourage the plant to grow more flowers. If you pick before any flowers go to seed, then the plant will put its energy into producing more flowers.

Dye notes

It's a pH sensitive dye and produces a range of shades from yellow to red depending on the acidity of the dye (see photo opposite). The flowers are spectacular in bundle dyeing (fresh or dry) and hammered onto fabric. For dye projects, see page 75 onwards.

Sulphur cosmos dye, unmodified

Fabric rinsed in water modified with bicarbonate of soda

Fabric rinsed in water modified with vinegar

These are some other kinds of cosmos which are beautiful for dyeing and deserve a mention.

Cosmos bipinnatus

Cosmos bipinatus is best used in bundle dyeing or hammering projects. The anthocyanins aren't very long-lasting, but they are stunning flowers to add to the garden and beautiful in floral arrangements.

Dark varieties such as 'Rubenza' (pictured below), 'Dazzler' and 'Carmine' make interesting prints on fabric. The pink/purple dye shifts to blue after washing due to a change in pH.

When growing cosmos, "pinch out" the tips, which means removing the growing tip of the plant with your finger and thumb. This encourages the plant to grow side shoots so it will end up as a bushier plant. It's worth doing this in the spring as you'll get more flowers.

GROW YOUR OWN COLOUR

Chocolate cosmos (Cosmos atrosanguineus)

Chocolate cosmos originates in Mexico and its flowers really do smell of chocolate. It's a tender perennial variety of cosmos that survives winter in zones 7 and above. In colder climates, the roots must be protected, or dug up and brought inside.

Up until now, it has only been propagated via tuberous roots, as the seeds were sterile. But very recently, seeds have been made available. They are expensive and difficult to germinate, so I bought a couple of ready-grown plants for my garden. In the future, I'll try growing them from seed!

The flowers are lovely to use in bundle dyeing and also hammered onto fabric.

Scabiosa atropurpurea

- Hardy annual
- Height: up to 1.2 m
- Planting distance: 45 cm
- Sow: Under cover in early spring or autumn, direct in mid spring
- Position: full sun
- Flowers: mid to late summer

Purple pincushion

Pincushion flowers (*Scabiosa atropurpurea*) are tall, willowy, relaxed flowers that look great in floral arrangements. The velvety dark purple petals of 'Black Knight' scabiosa are rich in anthocyanins and some of the flowers do appear almost black!

The flower heads hold dozens of tiny petals which each contain rich dye. The dark flower heads are scattered with white stigmas that look like little pearls. When a scabiosa flower goes to seed, the head is covered in little spikes and you can see why it's also called a 'pincushion'.

I first discovered the incredible dye potential of Black Knight scabiosa via Liz Spencer (The Dogwood Dyer), who learnt from natural dyer Kristin Morrison from Love All Species.

Photo below: *pH modified dye. Teal on left was unmodified. Lilac in centre was modified with vinegar. Green on right was modified with bicarbonate of soda.*

Growing

You can start the seeds off in early spring or early autumn, grow them in module trays, with a few seeds per module, covered with a fine layer of compost. Thin so there's only one seedling growing in each module. Then plant into the garden when it's warmer. Keep autumn-sown seeds in a cold frame or greenhouse over winter, and plant the following spring. Read pages 14-17 for detailed notes on growing from seed.

Harvesting

The more you pick, the more flowers you'll get, so harvest them regularly to get the most out of your plants. They are spectacular when used fresh; the petals are so juicy.

If you'd like to dry them for later, you can enjoy the flowers in a vase indoors and just as the flowers begin to go over, snip off the heads and dry them on a tray.

Dye notes

Fresh scabiosa petals make striking prints when hammered onto fabric. The tiny flowers can be flattened between two layers of fabric and pounded (see page 111 for the method). It's amazing to see how much dye each one contains.

As with all anthocyanin dyes, it's pH sensitive. Colours range from pink to purple, green to grey, and the shades depend on the acidity of the water, as well as dissolved impurities in your particular water supply.

The petals make spectacular ink for painting on paper (shown on opposite page and method described on page 101).

Above: *Purple pincushion flowers hammered onto cotton.*

Ink made from purple pincushion flowers & pH modified.

unmodified

+ vinegar

+ baking soda

Hollyhock

Alcea rosea

- Biennial
- Height: 1.5 - 2.5 m
- Planting distance: 45 cm
- Sow: Under cover in spring or direct in late summer or early autumn
- Position: sun
- Flowers: mid to late summer

Hollyhocks are perhaps one of the most quintessential English cottage garden plants, but did you know that this plant has exotic origins? It originates in the Middle East and was introduced in England in the sixteenth century.

Growing

It's a biennial which means it lives two years: the first year it grows leaves and establishes its roots, and is unlikely to flower strongly, if at all. Then in the second year it will grow a statuesque spear of flowers that stretch towards the light.

When you've grown hollyhocks in your garden once, they are likely to self-seed everywhere, even in cracks between paving stones.

Black hollyhock seeds are available in a double flower variety, and whilst they are beautiful and offer more dye material, the frilly flowers aren't as accessible for pollinators.

Hollyhocks don't transplant well; if the roots are disturbed, this will stop the plants growing. Sow seeds in paper pots or cardboard tubes, two seeds per pot, and remove the weaker seedling. Read pages 14-17 for detailed notes on growing from seed. When you plant them in the garden, dig a large enough hole to bury the entire paper pot. This way the roots are not disturbed. The tall flower stems can topple over in a windy spot, so may need support.

Harvesting

Pick flower heads every couple of days. Either use them fresh, or dry and store for the winter. You can also press them for bundle dyeing.

Dye notes

The dark flowers are rich in anthocyanins and the dye is pH sensitive. The fabric is grey/black in the dye pot, rinses to a teal blue in tap water, and can be shifted to a soft lilac with a rinse in vinegar water.

Hollyhock dye modified with vinegar on the right and unmodified on the left.

GROW YOUR OWN COLOUR

Japanese indigo

Persicaria tinctoria, also known as Japanese Indigo or Dyer's Knotweed, is a frost-tender member of the knotweed family. This semi-tropical plant likes a lot of sun. It can be grown from seed to flower in the spring through to autumn, and it dies when the temperatures drop later in the year.

We will be using the "salt rub" method which involves rubbing salt into fresh leaves, and rubbing the juicy mixture into fabric. This technique originates in Japan and is an easy way for growers to use indigo on a small scale. I learnt about this method in a You Tube video by the film maker Ryoya Takashima, where he visited the Ohara Koubou dye studio in Kyoto, Japan.

Try growing Japanese indigo on a small scale to get a taster for this incredible dye plant, and subsequent years you might choose to grow more plants from your saved seeds. You can dye a tiny scarf with just a handful of leaves or scale up.

Growing

Start your plants indoors, and once the risk of frost has passed, grow your plants in larger pots or plant in the ground.

Start your seeds in the mid spring and drop 5-6 seeds into little plant pots filled with compost. I learnt this 'multi-sowing' method (several seeds per pot) from no-dig gardening expert Charles Dowding.

He uses this method for growing vegetables and herbs, and it works well for Japanese indigo too!

The seeds need warmth and light to germinate, so put the tray of paper pots in a clear plastic bag to make a mini 'greenhouse', with some holes for air flow. Then place the tray on a warm windowsill or use a heat mat. This creates a warm, moist microclimate. A heat mat helps the seeds germinate quicker, but isn't absolutely necessary. On a windowsill, it can take 3-4 weeks for the seeds to sprout, but on a heat mat it will be much quicker. Fresh seeds give the best germination rates.

Once the seeds have started to sprout, remove the plastic bag and ensure the seedlings get as much light as possible. Keep indoors as frost will kill these tender

Persicaria tinctoria

- Tender annual
- Height: 90 cm
- Planting distance: 10 cm or further apart if multi-sown (several plants per pot)
- Sow: under cover in mid spring
- Position: full sun
- Harvest: several times through growing season

plants. Once the plants have grown an inch or two, 'pot on' into larger pots with more compost. Keep nurturing them with regular water and plenty of sunlight.

In the UK, I wait until the end of May or even the beginning of June before I plant them in the garden. My last frost date is at the end of March, but night-time temperatures continue to be quite low. In warmer climates, you will be able to plant yours out earlier. Choose a sunny position for your plants – ideally somewhere that gets sun most of the day.

When you plant your indigo babies outside, make a hole with a 'dibber' or a small trowel, and bury the plants so the stems are below the soil level and just the leaves are exposed. Water the plants well and they should now grow happily in their new home.

They are quite a demanding plant, and grow best with regular watering. As warmth-loving plants, they grow even better in a greenhouse or poly tunnel. If you grow "under cover" then you can plant them out earlier as they will be more protected from the cold and wind.

George Fukuda, from Bailiwick Blue Indigo Farm tells us, *"While indigo grows adequately outdoors in the UK, like most plants, warmer surroundings encourage faster growth. Tended in the right way, a healthier plant will give greater output; in the case of indigo this means more foliage. Persicaria tinctoria is a lover of water and is known to grow on river banks in the humidity of Asian summers. Growing under cover therefore controls this element by holding in humidity."*

Dyeing

After a couple of months, when you start to see some good growth, you can take your first harvest. When you cut the stems, this stimulates the plant to grow more, just like when you cut herbs. Dye with the leaves before they flower, as after this point they contain less indigo.

For your first project, choose something small such as a scarf, handkerchief, swatch of fabric or other small item like a baby hat. It must be made from natural fibres, although a tiny percentage of elastane is fine.

If you're dyeing wool or silk (animal protein fibres) then you can just wash and dye the fibres. For cellulose fibres such as cotton, linen or hemp, it's best to pretreat in soya milk. The protein acts as a binding agent between the fibre and dye, helping you achieve darker colours and improving colour fastness. This isn't needed for indigo vat dyeing, but here we are using a method with fresh leaves, which is different.

Prewash your fabric

Simply wash the fabric at 40°C in the washing machine with natural laundry liquid.

Pretreat fabric in soya milk

When dyeing cellulose fibres, follow the soya milk pretreatment method on page 85.

Dye your fabric

Cut a few stems from your plants. In the past I've done this with as little as 5g of leaves and dyed a baby hat. Whatever quantity you pick will be worth it for a pretty blue hue.

Remove the leaves from the stems and drop them into a bowl. Ideally use a bowl that's not used for food, as this is best practice for any natural dyeing, and the bowl may get stained if there are any scratches in the glaze. Read the other safety guidelines on page 76.

You can weigh your leaves. It doesn't matter how many you have, but it's interesting to know the amount for comparison purposes for next time.

Now comes the fun part. Either wear some rubber gloves (thin ones give you the best dexterity) or just accept that

you'll have blue hands for a few days!

Add salt to your bowl of fresh leaves. When I have less than 50g of leaves, I usually start with 1 teaspoon of salt. You will need more salt for more leaves. Then start scrunching the leaves in your hands and the leaves will begin to shrink immediately. In a short while you should begin to notice some frothy green juice dripping out of your hands. If the leaves still feel dry, then add another teaspoon of salt to the mixture and keep scrunching and rubbing. Keep doing this until you have a wet, dripping ball of green leaves.

Then add your dry fabric to the bowl. The juice will immediately stain the fabric green. Begin to massage the leaves into the fabric and the colour will start to turn more of a teal. Keep rubbing, massaging,

and continually move the fabric in your hands to try to get an even colour all over.

Carry on massaging and scrunching the leaves into the fabric until there is no more juice.

Depending on how many leaves you used in relation to the amount of fabric, your result may be mottled. In this case, you could pick some more leaves and even out the colour, or just accept your naturally 'marbled' pattern. If you start with damp fabric, this may also give a more even colour, as it helps the dye spread out more.

Notice how the colour deepens after a short while – this is the indigo oxidising. It will become even more blue after rinsing later.

Rinse out the chlorophyll

Let the fabric dry for the rest of the day or until the morning, then rinse in a bowl of water. The water will turn bright green as the chlorophyll washes away. You'll be left with a pretty shade of pale blue/teal.

Make patterns

When you have only a few leaves, scrunch the leaves and dab on fabric to make a pattern. Much like sponge painting that you might have done as a child, you can make mottled prints on fabric with a ball of squished indigo leaves.

Paint with indigo juice

Try painting with the juice from the scrunched leaves. When you add salt to your bowl of leaves and begin squeezing, notice how the mixture becomes very juicy. Instead of adding fabric at this point, pour off some of the juice and use it as paint! It works well on paper and fabric (silk or soya-treated cellulose).

Regrow the stems

You can make more plants from your cut stems by putting them in water. When they have started to root, plant them alongside your other indigo plants in the garden, and you'll soon have more leaves to harvest.

Save seeds

Depending on your climate, the flowering season for your plants will vary. In the UK, *Persicaria tinctoria* flowers in the late autumn and the seeds are ready to collect in October. Sometimes the flowers haven't matured enough before the first frost, so I have successfully picked the flower stems, placed in jars of water and brought them indoors.

When it comes to collecting seeds, look for shiny dark brown seeds, then snip off the whole top of the plant. You can then gently run your fingers along the flower heads to release the seeds.

DYE PROJECTS

Safety guidelines for dyeing

Here are some guidelines to keep in mind for any dyeing projects. This is not an exhaustive list so please also use your common sense.

- The book is about growing your own plants for dyeing, but if you choose to pick any wild plants, then take care when identifying anything and if you need help, consult a reliable book or a knowledgeable friend. Remember that some plants are toxic, so only dye with plants that you can correctly identify. Be extra cautious when children are helping.

- Use a separate set of equipment reserved for dyeing – not your kitchen pots, sieve, wooden spoons etc.

- When you are heating dye pots, make sure you have good air flow. Keep a window open and don't stand over a steaming pot and breathe in the vapour.

- Wear gloves to protect your skin from dyes.

- Wear thick gloves when opening steaming pots, as the steam can scald your wrists quickly.

- Keep dyes away from children, pets and food.

- Carefully label any jars of dye and ink that you store in the fridge so that everyone knows it's not edible! Do the same for dye that you freeze.

- Wear a dust mask when working with any mordant powders to protect your nasal passages, throat and lungs. Wear rubber gloves to protect your skin. Follow the safety information that is supplied when you buy mordants.

Photo opposite: French Marigold (left), Dyer's coreopsis (right)

Pre-washing or scouring fibres

The first step in the dyeing process is to thoroughly clean your fabric. This needs to be done before you mordant. The fibres need to be washed to remove any dirt, naturally occurring oils and other residues from the manufacturing process. You can usually tell when fabric will benefit from a good scour as the fabric is unbleached and it looks quite "raw". When fabric contains oils and other residues, the dyes will try to attach to grease or other coatings, rather than the actual fibres underneath. Then when the fabric is washed after dyeing, the dye will wash away as the coatings on the fabric are eventually cleaned off.

The standard way of cleaning **cellulose fibres** is to scour and you'll find a recipe for this on page 79 (opposite). When fabric is sold as "ready to dye" I personally don't always scour, as the fabric has already been cleaned. Also, it can be harsh on some delicate fibres. In these situations, I simply clean the fabric in the washing machine with laundry liquid. However, it's a personal choice and you may choose to scour everything. For thicker fabric, such as unbleached cotton canvas, I always recommend scouring as the fabric contains oils and grease, and without a proper scour, the mordants and dyes will not penetrate through to the fibres, so you'll end up with a patchy and pale result.

Raw silk contains a gum called sericin and this needs to be removed from the fibres before dyeing. For simplicity, that is not covered here and I recommend choosing silk that is "ready to dye", i.e. not raw silk. Simply hand wash "ready to dye" silk with a natural laundry liquid, rinse well, then move onto mordanting and/or dyeing.

Scouring cellulose fibres

Safety: Soda ash is highly alkaline and will irritate your skin. Wear gloves when handling soda ash or fabric that's been in soda ash solution.

1. Fill a large dye pot with water.

2. Next add the soda ash powder. Use 1-2 teaspoons soda ash per 4.5 litres water. Measure the amount of soda ash you'll use, and add to a small jar of luke warm water. Mix well, then pour this mixture into your large pot of water.

3. Add the fabric and simmer on the stove for 1-2 hours. Stir and rotate the fabric with a wooden spoon every so often to release air bubbles.

4. Then give the fabric a thorough rinse in the sink (wearing gloves to protect your skin) and discard the dirty liquid from the pot.

5. Move onto mordanting with alum or pretreating with soya milk.

Cleaning fabric in the washing machine

If you choose not to scour your fabric, then pre-wash it in the washing machine to try to get it as clean as possible.

Wash with a natural laundry detergent. Rinse thoroughly and then move onto mordanting or pretreating your fibres.

Mordanting & pretreating

What is a mordant and how is it different to pretreating in soya milk? Let's look at a few options for preparing fibres before dyeing.

Even though fibres will dye to some extent without any kind of mordant, it can be beneficial to either mordant with alum or pretreat with soya milk, as you will get darker and longer-lasting colours. You can see some colour comparisons on pages 82-83.

Protein vs cellulose fibres

Animal protein fibres have a natural affinity with plant dyes and readily absorb colour. Cellulose (plant) fibres don't have the same kind of affinity; without mordanting or pretreating, you will get much paler results that wash out quickly. Furthermore, many dyers still choose to mordant animal fibres to further improve colour fastness.

Alum vs soya milk

The most common way to mordant cellulose fibres is with alum, in the form of various compounds such as aluminium sulphate or aluminium acetate. These are said to produce the most colourfast results.

However, for many years I've been using a different method which involves treating fibres in diluted soya milk. Soya protein acts as a binding agent and effectively transforms cellulose fibres into protein-like fibres, so they take on some of the same properties. The dyes then bond to the soya protein coating that's on the fibres. I like this method because it's non toxic and I can do it in the kitchen with my children helping.

Making an informed decision

The type of mordant we choose depends on our priorities. My main focus is to work with non toxic, food-grade ingredients as much as possible. This is the driving force behind my textiles practice. However, I still use alum on occasions, especially when bundle dyeing, as the results with alum are much brighter and clearer. This isn't to say that you can't bundle dye with soya milk treated fabric, but if you compare results, you will probably find that alum gives you bolder results. Our priorities might be different for different projects. I think it's important to understand the different options, so we can make an informed decision for our projects.

Choosing a mordant that's right for you

Would you like the safest, least toxic method, especially if you'll be doing projects with children?

- Use soya milk on cellulose fibres (recipe on page 85)
- Dye silk with no mordant: silk is a protein fibre and has a natural affinity to plant dyes, so a mordant isn't absolutely necessary.

Is colour durability the most important factor for you?

- Use one of the tried-and-tested mordanting recipes with alum, such as aluminium sulphate on silk (page 88), aluminium acetate on cellulose (page 92), or tannin followed by aluminium sulphate on cellulose (recipe on page 90). The recipes in this book are just the tip of the iceberg when it comes to mordanting and there are many other possibilities. For further reading, take a look at *The Art & Science of Natural Dyes* by Boutrup & Ellis (2018).

Are you looking for the most environmentally friendly option?

- Aluminium lactate is deemed the most environmentally friendly form of alum, as it's a bi-product of the sugar and starch industry (recipe on page 92).
- A alternative to using soya milk (which is often imported), is to make your own local plant-based milk. Admittedly, soya protein is thought to have superior properties for binding dyes, but I've had good results with other types of milk too. For example, if you have a particular type of nut that you can forage e.g. almond, hazelnut or acorn, then make your own nut milk.
- Use any excess animal milk that you have at home and replace this for soya milk in the recipe on page 85.
- Instead of soya milk, collect the water left over from packets of tofu, or rinse out yogurt pots and use this 'rinse' liquid. If you do this, you can collect small amounts over time and freeze until you have enough. Simply pour into a container and store in the freezer, and keep adding to it over time.
- If you are keen to use soya milk, then you can source dried organic soya beans and make your own milk, or you can even grow soya beans in your garden.

Safety notes for using mordant powders

Wear a dust mask when working with any mordant powders to protect your nasal passages, throat and lungs. Wear rubber gloves to protect your skin. Follow the other safety guidelines on page 76.

Different mordants, fabrics & plants

	Sulphur cosmos		African marigold		Dyer's chamomile	
	cotton	silk	cotton	silk	cotton	silk
Soya milk + ferrous sulphate						
Soya milk						
No mordant						
A. Sulphate						
A. Acetate						
A. Lactate						

Note: A = Aluminium.

cotton   silk   cotton   silk   cotton   silk

Soya milk + ferrous sulphate

Soya milk

No mordant

A. Sulphate

A. Acetate

A. Lactate

Hopi Black Dye
sunflower seeds

Dyer's coreopsis

Purple pincushion flowers

GROW YOUR OWN COLOUR

Pretreating cellulose fibres in soya milk

This is a non toxic way to prepare your fibres before dyeing. Soya (soy) milk can be used as a pretreatment on fabric, acting as a binding agent between plant fibres and plant dyes. Soy protein binds to cellulose fibres, making fibres more receptive to plant dyes. This improves colour fastness and helps achieve darker dye colours.

The following recipe pretreats up to 400g of fabric. Buy soya milk that contains as few additives as possible. The recipe below uses store bought milk; homemade soya milk is more concentrated so will need to be diluted further. The aim is to coat the fibres with several layers of diluted milk – a thick layer will lead to uneven dyeing results later on.

Try to do this on a cool day so the milk stays as fresh as possible. Discard the milk if it goes off. This is a summary of the method from *Botanical Colour at your Fingertips* (2016).

Method

1. Pour 1 litre of soya milk into a bucket and add 5 litres of water. Mix well, then add your clean fabric in there and mix well. If the fabric isn't fully submerged, add more water. Leave to soak for 12 hours, and ideally mix it a few times.

2. Remove fabric, then squeeze out the milk. Spin out the excess liquid in the washing machine (spin cycle with no water). Hang to dry.

3. Dip the fabric in the bucket of milk again so it receives an even coating, squeeze by hand, then spin out the excess liquid in the washing machine. Allow to dry.

4. Do a final dip in the milk, squeeze out, then spin out in the washing machine. Use a quick wash cycle to clean your empty machine.

5. Leave the fabric to dry then set aside for a week before dyeing so the soy protein can cure on the fabric.

Pot as mordant method

If you decide to use the soya milk pretreatment method, then an aluminium pot is a useful tool for your dyeing. If you avoid alum, that doesn't mean that you can't benefit from the mordanting action of aluminium. It's possible to use an aluminium dye pot and have a similar, albeit, weaker effect.

Stainless steel pots are non reactive and perfectly fine for natural dyeing; in fact stainless steel is favoured by most natural dyers who work with alum. But if you choose to use the soya milk pretreatment method on fabric, then an aluminium pot is a useful tool.

Since we need to use a dye pot of some sort, we may as well choose one that's made from a "useful" metal. This is why I like to use aluminium for most of my dyeing. I don't cook food in aluminium because it's a reactive metal; whatever is cooked in the pot will most likely contain trace amounts of aluminium, and it's not healthy to ingest this metal. However, the reactive nature of aluminium is a useful feature for dyeing. This mordanting technique is called "pot-as-mordant".

The "pot-as-mordant" method is where we carry out the mordanting in the dye pot, at the same time as dyeing. Typically, dyers treat fibres with some form of alum before dyeing, which is called pre-mordanting. For a long time now, I've been pretreating fibres in soya milk, then I use an aluminium pot to dye fibres.

An aluminium pot isn't as effective as using alum, as the mordanting action is more random. Some of the dye particles are attracted to the sides of the pot, rather than the fabric. However, I find that using an aluminium pot makes enough of a difference to be worthwhile and I've continued to use this method for years. Also the brightening effect of using an aluminium pot cannot be dismissed. The dye colours speak for themselves!

A note on 'Time'

I always suggest dyeing fibres slowly, to achieve deeper and longer-lasting colours. Don't just dye for an hour, then rinse; gently heat fibres for longer periods of time, then leave fibres soaking and reheat on and off. Sometimes I allow fabric to soak for days at a time, but in these situations it's impossible to achieve even colours. This is why I like to use scrunch dyeing techniques (see page 96) and embrace the uneven way the fabric dyes. To sum up, *time* is an important factor in natural dyeing.

*Pouring water into an aluminium pot
containing French marigolds.*

Mordanting silk in aluminium sulphate

This is a simple one-step process for mordanting silk. You can use aluminium sulphate on cellulose too, but you'll need to pretreat the fibres with tannin first (see page 90).

Most mordants are calculated from a percentage of the *weight of fibre*, which we abbreviate as WOF. WOF refers to the dry weight of fabric (or yarn) to be mordanted. A digital kitchen scale is useful for weighing fibres and mordant powders.

What you need

- Aluminium sulphate
- A glass jar & small spoon
- A large lidded pot or bucket & large spoon for stirring

The method

1. Weigh your dry fabric and calculate 12% of that weight. That is how much aluminium sulphate you need. Use 12% of the weight of the fibre (WOF). For 100g fibres, you need 12g aluminium sulphate.

2. Soak the fabric for a few hours.

3. Safety: wear a face mask to protect your lungs from fine powders and wear gloves to protect your skin.

4. Put your glass jar onto your scales, zero the scales, then measure the amount of aluminium sulphate powder that you need from your earlier notes (12% WOF). Add some boiling water to the jar and stir well to dissolve.

5. Fill a large pot or lidded bucket 3/4 of the way to the top with warm water and pour in the jar of mordant mixture. Stir well.

6. Add the pre-soaked fibres to the pot. Make sure there's enough water to cover your fibres and they can move around easily. Add more water if necessary. Stir continually for the first few minutes, then stir every half an hour or so.

7. Leave the fabric in the pot for at least 6 hours, but it can be longer than this. Try to remember to stir gently from time to time. Leave a lid on the pot.

8. Wearing gloves, take the fibres out of the pot, rinse in cool water and then do a cool wash with a pH neutral laundry detergent.

9. Dry the fibres for later use or move straight onto dyeing.

Mordanting cellulose fibres in aluminium sulphate

Following on from the previous recipe, aluminium sulphate can also be used to mordant cellulose fibres, but the fibres need to be pretreated in tannin first.

When a cellulose fibre is treated with tannin, an insoluble compound is formed when the textile is exposed to the mordant, fixing both in the fibre. This enables the alum to bond more readily with the cellulose fibres, which gives better dye results later on.

Tannin has an affinity with all fibres; it can be used as a mordant on its own, or it can be used as an assistant with alum.

To summarise: mordanting cellulose in aluminium sulphate is a two step process: the first step is the tannin treatment, and the second step is the application of the alum mordant.

Tannins: gallnuts (oak galls) on the left, gallnut extract in middle, and myrobalan extract on the right.

What you need

Choose a "clear" or light coloured tannin, as darker tannins will colour the fibres and affect the final result. These are some options for clear tannins. (Boutrup & Ellis, 2018).

- Ground gallnuts at 20-30% WOF
- Tannin extract (e.g. gallnut or myrobalan) at 10% WOF
- Tannic acid at 20-30% WOF

Step 1: Treat cellulose fibres in tannin

1. If you're using gallnuts, then you need to first extract the tannins. Crush up the gallnuts, put in a dye pot and cover with water. Simmer the pot for an hour, then leave to cool for several hours. Strain out the gallnuts. This is your tannin solution.

2. Fill a large pot or plastic bucket with hot water.

3. If you're using tannin extract or tannic acid, then add the powder to the water and stir well to dissolve. If you're using gallnuts, then pour your tannin solution into the bucket of hot water and stir well.

4. Add your damp fibres into the tannin bath and push below the surface of the liquid. The fibres need enough space to move freely. Top up the water level if necessary.

5. Soak the fibres in the tannin bath for a couple of hours, stirring every so often to encourage the fibres to absorb the tannins as evenly as possible. The liquid will cool during this process and there's no need to reheat it. High temperatures will oxidise the tannins and potentially cause the fibres to dye darker than we want for this process. We are aiming for as little colour as possible on the fibres.

6. After a couple of hours, wear rubber gloves and remove the fibres from the tannin bath and squeeze the excess liquid back into the dye pot. The tannin bath can be reused.

7. Rinse the tannin-soaked fibres lightly. Don't rinse thoroughly as some of the tannin will be lost.

8. Then move straight onto the next step.

Step 2: Mordant fibres in aluminium sulphate

Follow the method used for mordanting silk on page 89.

Mordanting cellulose fibres in aluminium acetate or aluminium lactate

Aluminium acetate is another option for mordanting cellulose fibres. Its primary use in natural dyeing is for printing, but it can also be used as a pre-mordant for dyeing.

When we mordant with aluminium acetate, there's an additional step that we need to carry out. At the end of the process, we need to soak the fibres in a bath of calcium carbonate (chalk), or wheat bran, which fixes the mordant onto the fibres. This process is called "dunging", because the original dunging solution was made from dried cow dung. The phosphates in the dung are the active ingredients, but today we can simply use chalk.

The benefit of aluminium acetate over aluminium sulphate is that aluminium acetate can be applied to cellulose fibres without pretreating with tannin, so you can get brighter and clearer colours, without the potential darkening effect of tannin.

Aluminium lactate is a new-ish product on the market and works in a similar way to aluminium acetate but dissolves more easily. So, in this recipe you can use either aluminium acetate or lactate. Aluminium lactate has the benefit of being more environmentally friendly; it's a bi-product from the sugar and starch industry. It's produced from lactic acid obtained by fermentation of renewable materials. Also, aluminium lactate doesn't smell strongly of vinegar like aluminium acetate, so I personally find it more pleasant to use.

Aluminium acetate and lactate can be also used to mordant silk, although aluminium sulphate is a cheaper option.

Safety notes: Aluminium acetate is a very fine powder and can easily waft in the air, so work outside if you can, and always wear a mask to protect your lungs. Also it smells strongly of vinegar and may irritate your throat and nose. Wear gloves to protect your skin Be just as cautious when using aluminium lactate.

What you need

- Aluminium acetate or aluminium lactate
- A glass jar & small spoon
- 2 large lidded pots or buckets & large spoon for stirring
- Calcium carbonate (chalk)

Step 1: Mordanting

1. Weigh your dry cellulose fibres and calculate 5% of that weight. That is how much aluminium acetate or aluminium lactate you need. Use 5% of that weight of the fibre (5% WOF). e.g. 5g of aluminium acetate or aluminium lactate per 100g of dry cellulose fibres. (Note: a higher % of alum will increase the depth of the dye colour).

2. Soak the fibres for a couple of hours.

3. Wear a face mask to protect your lungs from fine powders and measure the amount of powder that you need (5% WOF) and put it in a glass jar. Then add 1 cup of water and stir to dissolve it. Use hot water for aluminium acetate and cold water for aluminium lactate, as aluminium lactate dissolves well in cold water.

4. Fill a large pot 3/4 of the way to the top with warm water and pour in the jar of mordant solution. Stir well.

5. Add the pre-soaked fibres to the pot. Make sure there's enough water to cover your fibres and they can move around easily. Add more water if necessary. Wearing gloves, mix the fabric with your hands to work the mordant into the fibres.

6. Stir the fabric from time to time, then leave it to soak in the pot over night. Keep a lid on the pot.

7. The next day, wearing gloves, take the fibres out of the pot and rinse in fresh water.

Step 2: "Dunging" in chalk

1. Calculate 5% WOF of calcium carbonate. So, for 100g fibres, use 5g calcium carbonate. Add this amount to a glass jar and mix with boiling water.

2. Fill a large pot or bucket with cool water. Then add the calcium carbonate mixture to this and stir well.

3. Put the fibres into the bucket of liquid. Wearing gloves, mix with your hands, then leave for around half an hour.

4. Remove, then rinse, as calcium carbonate can change the pH of the fibres.

5. Dry the fibres for future use, or move straight onto dyeing.

Sulphur cosmos dye

*A simple
dye pot recipe*

GROW YOUR OWN COLOUR

This is a simple and intuitive recipe for dyeing with your garden flowers. Read the additional notes for each of the dye plants earlier in the book; the individual plant profiles are on pages 32 - 65. You can also use this recipe with any wild dye flowers; my favourites include gorse, buddleja, goldenrod and hawthorn blossom.

What you need

- Fabric or an item of clothing made from natural fibres e.g. cotton, linen, hemp, viscose, silk.
- A metal pot with a lid. Use aluminium for its brightening effect and mordanting benefits (see page 86) or use stainless steel.
- Your choice of dye flowers.
- A sieve, muslin cloth and bowl for straining dye.

Scouring & mordanting

1. Scour or simply pre-wash your fabric (see page 78 for instructions).
2. Pretreat or mordant your fibres (see page 80 for help deciding which mordant to use).

Extracting dye

1. As a general guide, use the same weight of fresh flowers as dry fibres, e.g. for 50g of dry fabric, use 50g of fresh flowers. In reality, I admit that I rarely weigh fibres and simply use what I have available, but a 1:1 ratio is a good starting point. For dried flowers, you can double this and use 2:1 ratio of plants to fabric to get a good depth of colour, but as dried flowers are a limited resource in the winter, you might decide that it's best to use your dried blooms for bundle dyeing instead (see page 116 for the method).

2. Put the flowers in your pot and cover with just enough water so the plants are submerged. Less water is best, so your dye is as concentrated as possible. As the flowers rehydrate and swell up, you might need to add more water.

3. Drop in a swatch of fabric so you can monitor the dye colour more easily.

4. Gently heat the pot for 20-30 minutes. The aim is to gently extract the dye rather than cook the plants, as intense heat can dull the dye colour. Flowers usually release their dye immediately and the dye will gradually darken.

5. After about half an hour, take a look at your dye bath and check the colour of the small piece of fabric. How dark is it? Now, allow the flowers to soak in the warm dye with the lid on. Then take a look in an hour or so. Has the dye darkened further? How does the piece of fabric look now? Reheat the pot if you like.

6. Remove the swatch of fabric from the dye and see if it oxidises in the air and darkens.

7. When you're satisfied with the colour, line a sieve with a muslin cloth (or similar lightweight fabric) and strain the dye into a bowl. The cloth will catch tiny pieces of plant matter, leaving you with a clear dye, which will give you the most even dye result later on.

8. Wash out the dye pot so there aren't any deposits of dye on the sides, as these will leave marks on your fabric. Then pour your dye back into the clean pot.

9. Now your dye is ready to use. Try to use it as soon as possible; the colour will continue to change as it oxidises. It will probably be fine if left over night, but you won't be guaranteed the same colour.

Dyeing your fabric

1. Heat the dye gently. Take your fabric or clothing and dampen it in water before carefully lowering into the warm dye. Damp fabric absorbs dye more evenly so you'll get a more uniform colour. Alternatively, use this scrunch dye technique:

   Scrunch dyeing: It's tricky to dye fabric or clothing an even colour, so you can try tie-dye techniques and embrace the way the dye naturally collects in the folds of fabric. One of my favourite ways is to scrunch fabric and secure it in position with elastic bands. Drop it into the dye pot scrunched up and dye will collect in the folds and a subtle 'marbled' pattern will develop.

2. Add extra water so the fabric is fully submerged under the dye. If there are folds of fabric above the dye level, these will often oxidise first and sometimes end up darker. Stir the fabric gently once it's in the dye and observe how quickly the fabric takes on the colour.

3. Heat gently for 20 - 30 minutes, stirring every so often.

4. Usually fabric will benefit from soaking in the dye for a while longer. There's always a risk that it will dye slightly unevenly with dye settling into creases, so if you'd like to avoid this, it's best to stir regularly, or use the scrunch dye method.

5. You can reheat again to see if this darkens the colour of the fabric – it usually does! Another option is to allow the fabric to soak in the dye for several hours. Sometimes dye will oxidise and you'll get a much deeper colour if it's given time to develop. As with cooking, there are no absolutes and you can experiment.

6. When you're happy with the depth of colour on the fabric, lift the fabric out of the dye and squeeze out the liquid, then hang to dry. Try to squeeze out as much dye as possible so it doesn't drip, as this can cause streaks to form.

Tagetes erecta dye

Linen & silk
dyed with
Tagetes erecta
flowers.

GROW YOUR OWN COLOUR

Rinsing out the excess dye

- Once dry, try to wait a few days (ideally a week) before rinsing the fabric as this helps the fibres retain more colour. You can of course rinse immediately, but my preference is to do it the slow way. When you rinse the excess dye, do this in a bowl of fresh water and keep swishing the fabric until no more dye rinses out. Then use another bowl of fresh water and repeat.

- Finally, wash with a natural, pH neutral washing liquid, air dry and enjoy your botanically dyed fabric or clothing!

Changing the colour by modifying the pH

- Many dyes are pH sensitive. You can rinse your dyed fabric in water that's been modified with either an acid or alkali. Simply add a splash of lemon juice or vinegar for acid, or a teaspoon of bicarbonate of soda (baking soda) for alkali. Rinse your clothing in this modified water to change the colour. You'll need to do this each time you wash your dyed clothing, as the colour will shift back after washing.

- You can also paint dyed fabric with acids and alkalis (pictured below). This won't permanently change the dye as it will shift again when it's washed, but it is fun to experiment and is especially exciting for children. Use a separate paint brush for each modifier so the pH levels are kept distinct.

Dyes from sulphur cosmos (below) and coreopsis (right). Lemon juice turns these dyes yellow and baking soda dissolved in water turns them orange/red.

Coreopsis
+ lemon juice

Coreopsis
+ baking soda

Coreopsis

Painting with petals

This is a simple and beautiful way to sample flower dyes. You can do this with any of your dye flowers, whether you have fresh blooms or dried petals. It's essentially a method for making a super concentrated pot of dye for painting. In the photo opposite, it's demonstrated with coreopsis.

What you need

- Flowers (fresh or dried)
- A few little bowls
- A spoon
- Lemon juice or vinegar
- Bicarbonate of soda (baking soda)
- Paintbrushes
- Paper for painting
- Optional: a sieve to strain out the petals

Method

1. Pick off the petals from a few dye flowers and drop them into a bowl. Pour a little hot water over the petals – just enough so the petals are covered. Mix well with your spoon and try to squash the petals to extract more colour. Leave for a little while to allow the colour to darken.

2. When you're happy with the depth of colour, you can just dip your brush into the liquid and begin painting. Or strain out the petals to leave a clear paint that's free of any petals.

3. Coreopsis dye is pH sensitive, so pour a little dye into a couple of the wells in a paint palette (or extra bowls) and add a squeeze of lemon juice or vinegar to one, and a sprinkle of bicarbonate of soda to another. Watch the dye colours change immediately. Use a separate paint brush for each colour so you don't contaminate the pH of the liquids.

4. Optional: Sprinkle a tiny amount of ferrous sulphate into one of the bowls of ink to darken. Follow the instructions on page 106 for darkening with iron.

Storing ink & dye for later

You can store dye in labelled jars in the fridge. Add a drop of tea tree essential oil to help preserve it, and discard if it goes mouldy. This is a way to store extra dye and ink if you have leftovers, but you'll get brighter colours if you make it fresh each time, either with fresh flowers from the garden or dried in the winter.

Making green

Green is one of the most elusive colours in natural dyeing. Whilst many plants are green, it's actually quite rare to make green in a dye pot. Here I'll show you a few ways to make green from your dye garden.

1. **Yellow African marigold flowers** give me green in both stainless steel and aluminium dye pots. I've made green from fresh and dried flowers on numerous occasions. I separate out the orange flowers and just dye with the two shades of yellow: the almost neon yellow ones and golden yellow blooms. When extracting the dye, initially it is yellow, and then it appears to oxidise and darken to green. Sometimes fabric initially dyes yellow, but after washing and drying, the colour shifts to green. I can't promise that you'll always make green, but it's worth trying. Water quality will have an effect and I can't say for certain what shifts the dye to green. I also made green from French marigolds at another home with different water, so both types of marigold are worth trying to see what colour you get.

2. **Purple pincushion flowers** also make green; see examples on pages 61 and 83.

3. **Over dyeing yellow with indigo** is the most reliable method for making green; the colour is more stable than the methods above. In the photo opposite, there are two shades that I made with fresh Japanese indigo leaves: one with the underlayer dyed with French marigolds and the other with dyer's chamomile. Compare these shades to the green that came straight from the dye pot from African marigolds which is much more of a 'grass' green.

    Here we are working with fresh indigo leaves, but you can take things a step further and extract the dye and store it as a pigment and make an indigo vat at any point of the year. That method is beyond the scope of this book. As a starting point, I recommend buying indigo pigment and looking up a recipe for an "indigo fructose vat". That's a really simple way to begin!

African marigold flowers

Dyed with dyer's chamomile flowers
followed by fresh Japanese indigo
leaves

Dyed with French
marigold flowers
followed by fresh
Japanese indigo
leaves

In each pile of fabric swatches, the one on the right was darkened with iron water.

Sulphur cosmos

African marigold

Dyer's chamomile

Hopi Black Dye sunflower

GROW YOUR OWN COLOUR

Darkening dyes with iron

Iron water is a handy tool in natural dyeing which you can use to darken dyes and paint patterns with a brush. It's simply rusty water. Depending on the dye, the colour will change more or less when it comes into contact with rust.

When dyes or dyed fabric interact with rust, the colours are instantly darkened; we say that iron "saddens" the dye. Iron is a mordant and improves colour fastness of dyes. Earlier in the book, I showed you how to pre-mordant with alum, and now we are going to use iron as a post-mordant. Dye your fibres then dip in iron water to change the colours. It's an incredibly simple way to widen your palette of colours.

Iron can degrade animal fibres, so it's best to use it very sparingly on silk. It doesn't have such a damaging effect on cellulose fibres.

Iron water is simply rusty water; it's orange in colour and smells rusty. You can buy a packet of iron crystals that you dissolve in water, or make your own rust water with pieces of metal.

Ferrous sulphate

Buy ferrous sulphate from natural dye supply shops. A little goes a long way, so a packet will last a long time.

Homemade iron water

Alternatively you can easily make your own iron water. Gather scrap pieces of rusty metal and place in a glass jar. Fill the jar with water and white vinegar (50/50 mix) and put the lid on. Over the course of a few weeks, the water will turn rusty. You'll know when your iron water is ready to use as the liquid will turn orange. Keep topping up the jar with pieces of metal as you find them over time. As you use iron water in your projects, you can top up with more water and vinegar. The strength of your iron water will increase over time.

Photo opposite: *Cotton fabric samples dyed with flowers. Within each pile, the fabric on the right has been darkened with iron water.*

Equipment & safety

Before we look at how to use iron water, these are a few important notes:

- Wear gloves when working with iron, as it can irritate your skin.

- Use a different set of equipment to your usual dye pots, bowl, sieve and spoons. Iron is hard to wash off equipment and then it can have a darkening effect on any dyes that you use in the future. So, it's best to reserve a bowl and spoon just for iron water.

- Never put iron into an aluminium pot as it can 'contaminate' it and future dyes may be darkened.

- Follow the other safety guidelines on page 76.

- To paint with iron water, you can use some kind of thickening agent to make the liquid more viscous. Some options include gum Arabic, guar gum and gum tragacanth (instructions on page 109).

Darkening dyes with iron water

1. Take your designated 'iron water' bowl and fill with plain water.

2. Wear rubber gloves to protect your skin.

3. If using **ferrous sulphate:** start by dissolving half a teaspoon of ferrous sulphate into the water and mix well. Observe the colour of the water and keep mixing. As you stir, it oxidises and rust forms. Once you see the water turn orange, your iron water is ready to use.

4. If you're using **homemade iron water**, then strain some of the liquid from your jar through a sieve into the bowl of water. It may not be very concentrated if it's a fairly new jar, so you might need to use a fair amount of it. If it's a very deep orange colour, then you won't need much.

5. Dampen your fabric in another bowl of plain water.

6. Get another bowl or bucket and fill it with water. This will be for rinsing the fabric after dipping in iron.

7. Wearing gloves, dip your dyed fabric into the bowl of iron water. Use your hands to work the iron water into the fabric so the colour changes evenly. Once you're satisfied with the colour and that it's darkened evenly, take it out and rinse in the other bowl or bucket of water.

8. Wash the fabric with pH neutral laundry liquid to remove the lingering smell of rust.

Dipping: you can put just one end of the fabric into iron water to create a two-tone effect.

Hopi Black Dye sunflower seeds

African marigold

Dyer's chamomile

Painting with iron water

1. Protect your table with a sheet of cardboard.

2. Take a small jar or bowl and fill with a few tablespoons of plain water.

3. If you're using **ferrous sulphate**, then sprinkle about a quarter teaspoon of ferrous sulphate crystals into the water and mix well. Keep mixing until the water has turned orange.

4. To paint with **homemade iron water**, simply strain out some of your liquid from your larger jar through a sieve into a small bowl.

5. Lay your fabric onto the cardboard that's resting on the table.

6. Take a paintbrush, dip into the iron water and simply paint onto your dyed fabric. Watch as the colour darkens instantly. Before you paint any clothing or more precious fabric, test on some scrap fabric. Try different paint brushes for different effects.

7. Allow your painted fabric to dry, then rinse in plain water and wash with pH neutral laundry liquid to remove the smell of rust.

Optional: Thickening iron water

To paint more precise lines, thicken the iron water with a little bit of gum Arabic, guar gum or gum tragacanth. These ingredients can also be used to thicken dyes. The gums make the water more viscous which means that painted patterns don't bleed into the fibres, so you can paint more detailed patterns.

Use:

*   4 teaspoons of iron water
*   1/4 teaspoon of gum of choice e.g. gum Arabic, guar gum or gum tragacanth

Add the powdered gum very slowly, sprinkling with your fingers, adding it bit by bit. Mix vigorously with a spoon or fork (dedicated to iron, never to be used in the kitchen again). Whisk the liquid and it will thicken. Paint a test line on some dyed fabric to see if the iron water is thick enough. You'll know that it's ready when the painted line doesn't bleed into the fabric. Too much gum will turn it to jelly, which won't work for painting. You can also gently heat the iron water to help dissolve the powders more easily.

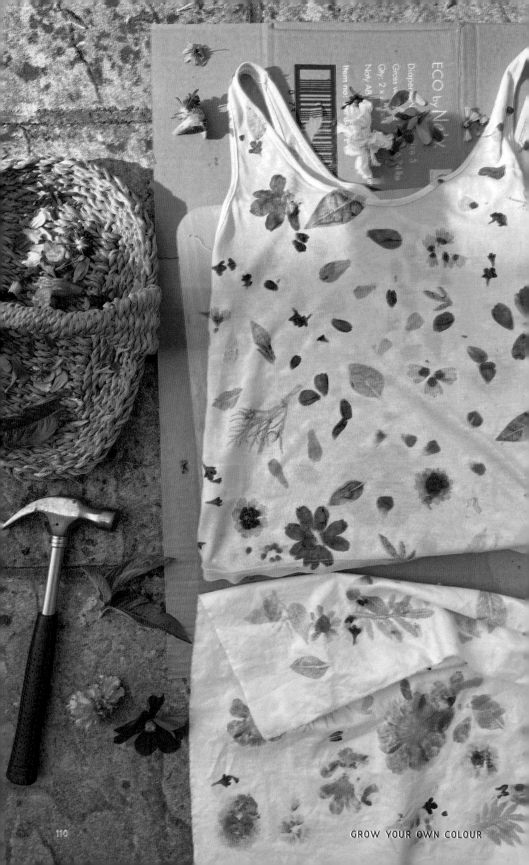

GROW YOUR OWN COLOUR

Flower pounding

Use this plant hammering method to create your own unique botanical prints. In this tutorial, I've printed a much-loved camisole top with coreopsis, cosmos, marigold petals, purple pincushion flowers and leaves from Japanese indigo. It's a simple way to bring life back into an old garment.

This technique is a way to enjoy an entire flower: the shape and the colour. The prints are mesmerising and a lot of detail is captured!

History of the technique

I learnt this method from Australian-based natural dyer Samorn Sanixay who generously shared the technique in my book called *Plant Dye Zine* (2020). Samorn has developed this method over the years and is skilled at creating long-lasting prints on fabric.

In *Plant Dye Zine*, Samorn tells us that this plant pounding technique can be traced back to different ethnic groups across the world. For example, in Indonesia they use young Indian almond and teak leaves to create spectacular red prints.

Samorn learnt the method from studying the work of Bettye Kimbrell (1936 - 2016) who was a quilter from Alabama, USA. In Bettye's biography, it says that she came across beautiful flower and leaf pounded quilts at a quilting fair and became fascinated by this technique which was inspired by Native American Cherokee people. Samorn has been experimenting with plant pounding for years and has developed special techniques.

What you need

- An item of clothing made from natural fibres (a small percentage of elastane is fine).
- An extra piece of fabric to lay on top.
- Fresh flowers and leaves.
- A hammer.
- A small, sturdy wooden board for hammering onto (small enough to slip inside your clothing, between the layers of fabric)

Scouring & mordanting

1. Scour or simply pre-wash your fabric (see page 78 for instructions).

2. Pretreat or mordant your fibres (see page 80 to decide which mordant to use). I pretreated this top in soya milk (see instructions on page 85), then waited a week before printing, which gives time for the soya protein to cure on the fibres.

Plant pounding

1. Gather your plants on a dry day. If they are wet, the flowers are likely to splatter when you hammer them, and the prints won't be as crisp.

2. Slip your wooden board between the layers of fabric of your clothing so you only hammer onto one layer of fabric at a time. Don't hammer directly onto concrete as this can make little holes in your fabric. You can lay a sheet of cardboard under the wood to absorb some of the impact and reduce the noise.

3. Lay your first flower onto the fabric and cover with an extra piece of fabric. You will get two prints with this method: one on the clothing and one on the top piece of fabric.

4. With careful and controlled hammering, begin pounding a flower. Watch as the print transfers to the layer of fabric above. Hammer all over the flower and continue until you can see the complete flower show through on the top piece of fabric. Hammer Japanese indigo leaves and see how the prints turn darker as they oxidise.

5. Remove the fabric and peel off the flower.

6. Continue hammering flowers, individual petals and leaves one at a time across your garment.

7. Keep printing until you have finished your design.

8. When you've finishing hammering all the flowers, allow the fabric to dry.

GROW YOUR OWN COLOUR

Heat-setting the prints

1. Once dry, try to peel off any plants that are still stuck on the fabric.

2. Give the whole garment a press with a hot iron all over to help set the dye.

Rinsing & washing

1. Rinse in cool water to remove the remaining leaves, petals and also to wash out the excess dye. If you use hot water, the anthocyanin pigments (red, pink and purple) may disappear, as this pigment isn't heat-stable, so avoid hot water.

2. When you wash with laundry liquid, the change in pH will alter many of the colours, which is all part of the natural process! Anthocyanins will turn from pink/purple to blue, and some of the yellow flowers will darken to orange.

Washing & caring for your clothing

Hand wash with a pH neutral washing liquid in cool water, and dry in the shade. The colour may shift and lighten over time. Enjoy the gradual change in the design, or hammer more plants if you like.

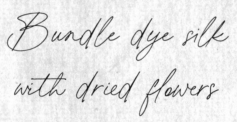

Bundle dye silk with dried flowers

Bundle dyeing is a simple way to make patterns on fabric. Simply scatter petals onto pre-mordanted fabric, roll, tie up, then steam. The steam transfers the dyes into the fibres. Unlike making a pot of dye, none of the dye is wasted in water, it transfers directly into the fabric.

Dye a silk scarf with dried flowers and bring some sunshine into the darker months. This technique works with any natural fibres using fresh or dried plants.

A bundle dye kit makes a fun present. I like to package up 'do-it-yourself' gifts containing white scarves and an envelope of dried homegrown flowers. I write out the simple directions on a card for the recipient to follow. See an example of a kit on page 130.

What you need

- A silk scarf or silk clothing
- String or ribbon for tying up the bundle
- A saucepan or pot with a lid
- A steaming insert to go inside the pot
- A spoon or tongs
- An extra piece of fabric to lay inside the steamer
- Dye flowers (fresh and/or dry)
- Optional: alum for mordanting silk.

Prewashing & mordanting

1. Pre-wash the silk (see page 78 for discussion on this).

2. Mordant your fibres (see page 80 to decide which mordant to use). I chose aluminium acetate for this scarf. As silk is a protein fibre, a mordant isn't absolutely necessary, but it will give darker, clearer prints.

Bundle dyeing

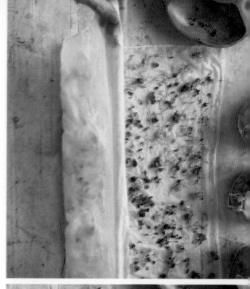

1. Gather your flowers.

2. Dampen the silk and place onto a clean table top. Spread out the fabric with your hands to smooth the wrinkles.

3. You will be laying your design onto half of the fabric, so find the centre.

4. Lay the dye materials onto the fabric making sure they are as flat as possible. You may have to take the flowers apart and arrange the petals. Mind the centre line to make sure there isn't a white stripe going through the middle of your fabric. Use more or less flowers for different effects. In this example, I was aiming for an entirely patterned scarf. But it's possibly even more beautiful with fewer flowers as there's contrast with the white background.

5. Once you're happy with the arrangement, fold the blank half of fabric over the half with the plants.

6. Use a piece of string or ribbon to tie up the bundle.

7. Roll your halved fabric up into a cylinder. It will look like a long sausage of fabric.

8. Begin rolling the sausage into a snail.

9. Wrap and lace the string around the bundle to tie it up.

GROW YOUR OWN COLOUR

Steaming your bundle

1. Fill your pot with water and place the steaming insert inside it. Make sure the water doesn't fill into the insert.

2. Lay a piece of fabric onto the steaming insert. This is to protect the fabric from burning when the metal heats up.

3. Turn your stove onto medium heat, then place the lid on the pot to let the steam begin to accumulate.

4. Once the condensation begins to gather on the inside of the lid, add your bundle into the pot.

5. Steam your bundle for about 20-25 minutes. Wearing gloves, check on it every so often. Use a spoon or tongs to carefully rotate and flip it. Keep an eye on the water level and add more water if needed.

6. After 20-25 minutes, let the bundle cool before handling, then cut or untie the string and unroll it.

7. Shake off the flowers and allow the scarf to dry fully.

8. Ideally wait a few days before rinsing.

9. Rinse with cool water, wash with natural laundry liquid, then hang to dry out of direct sunlight.

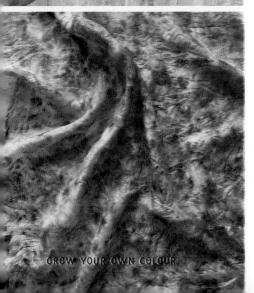

Bundle dye cotton with flowers

Bundle dye with your fresh garden flowers through the summer and autumn. You can dye any natural fibres and here I have bundle dyed a cotton t-shirt. Bring some life back to your old clothes or search for white clothes in secondhand shops.

What you need

- Clothing or fabric made from natural fibres (a small percentage of elastane is fine)
- String or ribbon for tying up the bundle
- A saucepan or pot with a lid
- A steaming insert to go inside the pot
- A spoon or tongs
- An extra piece of fabric to lay inside the steamer
- Dye flowers from your garden (fresh and/or dried)
- Your choice of mordant

Scouring & mordanting

1. Scour or simply pre-wash your fabric (see page 78 for instructions).

2. Pretreat or mordant your fabric (see page 80 to decide which mordant to use). I mordanted this cotton t-shirt in aluminium acetate as this method gives clearer prints than the soya milk pretreatment method that I usually favour.

Bundle dyeing

1. Gather flowers from your garden.

2. Dampen the fabric and place onto a clean table top. Smooth out the fabric with your hands to try to remove the wrinkles.

3. Find the centre of your t-shirt, since you will be laying your design onto half of the fabric.

4. Lay the flowers onto the fabric making sure they are as flat as possible. You may have to take some of the flowers apart (e.g. marigold and scabiosa) and sprinkle petals. Mind the centre line to make sure there isn't a white stripe going through the middle of your t-shirt. Use more or less flowers for different effects. You can also include some dried flowers if you like.

5. Once you're happy with the arrangement, fold the blank half of the t-shirt over the half with the plants.

6. Place more flowers onto the back half of the t-shirt.

7. Use a piece of string or ribbon to tie up the bundle.

8. Roll your halved t-shirt up into a cylinder. It will look like a sausage of fabric. If you like, you can tuck in extra flowers as you roll up the fabric.

9. Begin rolling the sausage into a snail.

10. Wrap and lace the string around the bundle to tie it up.

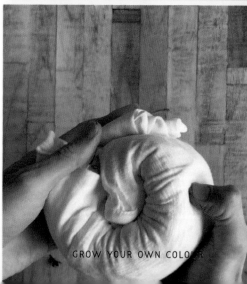

GROW YOUR OWN COLOUR

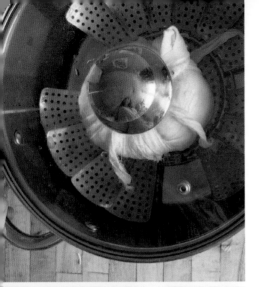

Steaming your bundle

1. Fill your pot with water and place the steaming insert inside it. Make sure the water doesn't fill into the insert.

2. Optional: Lay a piece of fabric onto the steaming insert before you put your bundle in there.

3. Turn your stove onto medium heat, then place the lid on the pot to let the steam begin to accumulate.

4. Once the condensation begins to gather on the inside of the lid, add your bundle into the pot.

5. Steam your bundle for about 20-25 minutes. Wearing gloves, check on it every so often. Use a spoon or tongs to carefully rotate and flip it. Keep an eye on the water level and add more water if needed.

6. After 20-25 minutes, let the bundle cool before handling, then cut or untie the string and unroll it.

7. Shake off the flowers and allow the fabric to dry fully.

8. Ideally wait a few days before rinsing.

9. Rinse with cool water and wash with natural laundry liquid. Some of the colours will shift with the pH change. Pink and purple cosmos prints (anthocyanins) will turn blue, yellow from coreopsis may darken to orange, and yellow from marigolds may turn green-ish.

10. Hang to dry out of direct sunlight.

NEXT STEPS

126

Caring for plant-dyed clothing

The flower dyes in this book are more delicate than some other natural dyes, so extra care must be taken to try to keep the shades as vibrant as possible. Out of all the plants, indigo is the most stable and long-lasting. Here are some general considerations for washing and caring for naturally dyed clothing.

Store out of sunlight

To preserve the colours from natural dyes for as long as possible, store out of sunlight when not in use. When you dry your clothing, hang in the shade.

Washing

Choose a natural laundry liquid that's pH neutral. Don't wash excessively or with harsh chemical products, as they may bleach your dyes.

If you modified the pH of your fabric to shift the colour, then you will need to rinse it in pH modified water each time it's washed to return the fabric to your desired shade. This can be a fun feature to work with, as some dyes are quite literally colour-changing. You can shift the colour each time you wash it and have a totally different look!

Living colours

Colours from plants are 'alive' in a way that synthetic dyes are not. If something fades, then you can over dye or top up the colour with more homegrown or foraged dye plants.

Testing colour fastness

The colour fastness of a dye tells us how well it withstands sunlight exposure, washing and rubbing.

To test light fastness

The purpose of a light fastness test is to see how quickly and to what extent sunlight fades a particular dye. Assessing light fastness involves exposing a portion of fabric (or yarn) to sunlight whilst keeping the rest of the sample out of the light. After a few weeks the colour of the uncovered and covered portions can be compared to see how much the dye has faded.

One way of doing this is to take a piece of cardboard and cut out a long slot, then tape fabric samples to the back of the card so that a portion is visible through the slot and the rest is hidden (pictured opposite). Then place the samples somewhere that is bright, but does not receive direct sunlight. For example, tape your samples to a wall adjacent to a north facing window (in the northern hemisphere). Then, take a look at the results after a month and assess the level of fading.

To test wash fastness

Before testing for wash fastness, it's important to first rinse the fabric or yarn thoroughly to remove any excess dye, otherwise the results may be misleading. To test for fading, simply take a piece of fabric or yarn and cut it in half. Put one half aside and wash the other half a few times. Then compare the two pieces to see how the colour has changed.

To test rub fastness

Simply rub samples of wet and dry fabric on undyed fabric to check for colour transfer.

Looking at your results

The results help us decide which dyes are best for which purpose. For example, dyes that aren't very light fast aren't suitable for dyeing cushions. This is particularly important if you sell your dyed items. However, for your own enjoyment purposes, this might not matter to you, and you can simply enjoy the colours then redye later.

Hopi black
sunflower seeds

Japanese indigo

*Setting up a
light fastness test*

Sulphur Cosmos

Hopi Black Sunflower

Purple Pincushion

Dyer's Coreopsis

African Marigolds

Dyer's Chamomile

French Marigolds

GROW YOUR OWN COLOUR

Buying seeds & flowers

Now we've reached the end of this book, you've seen a selection of dye flowers that you can add to your garden. Even if you don't have time for any dye projects over the next few months, it's still rewarding to see the plants grow and you can enjoy them in floral arrangements, then dry the flowers when they go over. Build up a stash and use them in projects over the winter, or even in the coming years.

Favourite shops for seeds & flowers

These are some shops that sell seeds and also dried flowers, so you can get started with some dye projects right away!

bailiwickblue.com (UK, seeds & flowers)

pigment.org.uk (UK, flowers)

chilternseeds.co.uk (UK, seeds only)

dyeing-crafts.co.uk (UK, seeds & flowers)

wildcolours.co.uk (UK, seeds & dye extracts)

thedogwooddyer.com (US, seeds & flowers)

grandprismaticseed.com (US, seeds only)

Buying mordants

These shops stock mordant powders (e.g. alum & ferrous sulphate), assists (e.g. chalk), as well as natural dyes:

wildcolours.co.uk (UK)

botanicalcolors.com (US)

maiwa.com (US)

Bibliography

ANDERSON, Tanya. 2021. *A Woman's Garden: Grow Beautiful plants and Make Useful Things*. Cool Springs Press.

BOUTRUP, Joy & ELLIS, Catharine. 2018. *The Art & Science of Natural Dyes: Principles, Experiments & Results*. Schiffer Publishing.

CARDON, Dominique. 2007. *Natural Dyes: Sources, Tradition, Technology and Science*. Archetype Publications.

CAUTHEN, Joyce H. 2013. *Out of Whole Cloth: The Life of Bettye Kimbrell*. Published by Joyce Cauthen.

DEAN, Jenny. 2010. *Wild Colour: How to grow, prepare & use natural plant dyes*. Octopus Books.

DESNOS, Rebecca. 2016. *Botanical Colour at your Fingertips*. Published by Rebecca Desnos.

DESNOS, Rebecca. 2020. *Plant Dye Zine*. Published by Rebecca Desnos.

DESNOS, Rebecca. 2022. *Plant Forage Make, volume 2*. Published by Rebecca Desnos.

DOWDING, Charles. 2007. *Organic Gardening: The natural no-dig way*. Green Books.

DOWDING, Charles. 2022. *No Dig: Nurture your soil to grow better veg with less effort*. DK.

DUERR, Sasha. 2020. Natural Palettes: Inspiration from Plant-Based Color. Princeton Architectural Press.

DUERR, Sasha. 2016. *Natural Color: Vibrant plant dye projects for your home and wardrobe*. Watson-Guptill Publications.

FOSTER, Claire & RUBER Sabina. 2019. *The Flower Garden: How to grow flowers from seed*. Laurence King Publishing.

GOUGH, Robert & MOORE-GOUGH, Cheryl. 2011. *The Complete Guide to Saving Seeds*. Storey Publishing.

HORTON, Helen. 2022. *'Planet friendly': RHS to no longer class slugs and snails as pests*. The Guardian Newspaper.

PROUST, Milli. 2022. *From Seed To Bloom: A Year of Growing & Designing with Seasonal Flowers*. Hardie Grant Quadrille.

RICHARDS, Huw. 2022. *The Vegetable Grower's Handbook*. DK.

Web: Last accessed on 13 September 2022.

- https://botanicalcolors.com/how-to-mordant/
- https://www.nativeseeds.org/pages/hopi-black-dye-sunflower
- https://www.grandprismaticseed.com/dye-plants/hopi-black-dye-sunflower
- https://www.dpi.nsw.gov.au/__data/assets/pdf_file/0020/41645/Soil_fungi.pdf
- Indigo film by Ryoya Takashima: https://www.youtube.com/watch?v=S94siuEEH7s

Thanks for joining me!

Let's keep in touch...

Join my mailing list for musings on plants,
creativity & simplicity:
rebeccadesnos.com/newsletter

Follow me on Instagram: **@rebeccadesnos**

Send an email: **info@rebeccadesnos.com**

Other titles published by Rebecca Desnos
available via rebeccadesnos.com

Picture credits in *Grow Your Own Colour.*

The publisher would like to thank the following for their kind
permission to reproduce their photographs:

Emily Quinton – portraits on pages 4 and 6.
Siobhan Watts – portrait on page 133.
Shutterstock – photos on pages 46, 59 and 65 (top left).

All other images are by Rebecca Desnos.

Join my online class...

There's a video workshop that accompanies this book with several projects... bundle dye with flowers, dye with fresh indigo, and hammer plants onto fabric. Sign up on **rebeccadesnos.com**

Printed in Great Britain
by Amazon

22971088R00080